THEODORA FITZGIBBON

A TASTE OF WALES

Welsh Traditional Food

Period photographs specially prepared by George Morrison

PAN BOOKS LTD

LONDON AND SYDNEY

First published 1971 by J. M. Dent & Sons Ltd
This edition published 1973 by Pan Books Ltd,
Cavaye Place, London SW10 9PG

ISBN 0 330 23624 5

2nd Printing 1973
3rd Printing 1974

© Theodora Fitzgibbon 1971

*For Margaret, Rosemary and Charles Leach, with
affection and many thanks for their kindness and help.
Also to the memory of Great-Aunt Polly Mary, and
my Mother*

Permission to reproduce the specially prepared photographs for
any purpose must be obtained from the author.

*Printed Offset Litho in Great Britain by
Fletcher & Son Ltd, Norwich*

ACKNOWLEDGMENTS

I wish to thank all the friends who have helped me in my research for this book, particularly Margaret, Rosemary and Charles Leach for the loan of family papers, photographs and books and for their most kind hospitality and encouragement. Also Donald and Patricia Moore for the loan of family manuscripts and their immense help in tracing certain photographs and providing me with invaluable contacts; Lieutenant-Colonel Llewelyn Evans of Bridgend, Glamorgan, for the loan of his remarkable photographs on pages 117 and 119, taken by him as a student, and for relating his personal memories, thus bringing the traditional ceremonies to life; not forgetting a fellow researcher, Walter Haydn Davies of Gilfach Bargoed, Glamorgan, who helped us to find an elusive photograph. My thanks are also due to the following people for their extreme kindness and help in the preparation of this book: Miss Megan Ellis, Keeper of Prints, Drawings and Maps, Miss Gwyneth Lewis, and Mr M. L. Timothy of the National Library of Wales, Aberystwyth, for their patience and valuable assistance; Miss B. Nelmes, Mr J. M. Davies and Mr Norman Lewis Thomas (who also allowed me to quote from his book, *The Story of Swansea's Districts and Villages*, 1969) of the Royal Institution of South Wales, Swansea, who went to great trouble for me; Mr Stanley Yonge, Mr L. M. Rees, Mrs S. Long of Swansea Central Public Library for their kind help; Mr J. E. Thomas, Mr E. H. Jones, and Mr T. J. Hopkins of Cardiff Central Public Library; Mr Cefni Barnett, Director of the Newport Museum and Art Gallery; Miss Hilary Thomas and particularly Mrs Patricia Moore of the Glamorgan Record Office, Cardiff, for photographs and manuscripts; Mr D. Morgan Rees, Keeper of Industry, National Museum of Wales, Cardiff; R. George Nicol, of the Royal Commission on Ancient and Historical Monuments in Wales and Monmouthshire;

Dr Ilid Anthony, St Fagans, Welsh Folk Museum; Mr M. J. Cullen, Celtic Press Ltd, Merthyr Tydfil, for the photograph on page 4; Mr and Mrs W. Howells, Dial Inn, Lamphey, Pembroke, for photographs; Mr and Mrs Evans of The Old Black Lion Hotel, Aberystwyth, who made our stay comfortable and lent me books; Bwrdd Nwy Cymru (Wales Gas Board) for allowing me to quote from their booklet; likewise the National Federation of Women's Institutes for giving me permission to quote from *Country Feasts and Festivals*, 1962.

I am also indebted to the Right Honourable Marchioness of Anglesey for her kindness and help; Mrs Eluned Roberts of Conway; Mrs G. Kybett of Hafod Arms Hotel, Devil's Bridge; Mrs T. Appleton, West House, Llantwit Major, and Mrs Eric Hicks, for their help in various ways; and finally Professor David Greene, Senior Professor of the Dublin Institute of Advanced Studies, and Donald Moore for their help with linguistic problems.

Photographs on pages 3, 7, 11, 15, 17, 19, 22, 25, 26, 29, 38, 40, 43, 45, 46, 49, 52, 61, 62, 64, 67, 70, 72, 79, 84, 91, 93, 96, 98, 102, 106, 112 are reproduced by kind permission of the National Library of Wales, Aberystwyth; on pages 37, 69, by kind permission of Swansea Central Public Library; on pages 14, 76, by kind permission of the Royal Institution of South Wales, Swansea; on pages 33, 51, 74, by kind permission of Cardiff Central Public Library; on page 11, by kind permission of the National Museum of Wales, Cardiff; on pages 34, 101, 110, by kind permission of Newport Museum and Art Gallery; on pages 55, 87, by kind permission of Glamorgan Record Office, Cardiff; on page 58, by kind permission of Royal Commission on Ancient and Historical Monuments in Wales and Monmouthshire,

Aberystwyth; on page 4, by kind permission of *Merthyr Tydfil Express*; on pages 9, 56, 83, 109, 114, by kind permission of Mrs C. E. Leach; on pages 31, 89, 95, by kind permission of Mr W. Howells; on pages 117, 119, by kind permission of Lieutenant-Colonel Llewelyn Evans; on page 8, by kind permission of Mrs C. S. Monson.

A special mention must be made of the photographs in this book taken by Henry Hussey Vivian (1821–94) (later first Baron Swansea) on pages 25, 40, 49, 61, 72, 98 and 106. At the age of nineteen he was responsible for importing the first photographic lens and camera from Paris to Wales (in 1840). The earliest photographs in this collection must have been taken with that apparatus. Some of these photographs (originally on paper negatives or 'calotypes', a process patented by W. H. Fox Talbot in February 1841 and called 'Talbotypes') have never before been published. The extreme beauty, lyrical quality and spontaneity of the family activities give them an historical significance, and I am deeply indebted to George Morrison for being able to reproduce them with such superb quality.

John Thomas (1838–1905) was born of a humble family at Glan-rhyd, Cellan, Cardiganshire. He started his working life selling stationery and postcards to newsagents. Finding the postcards scant in Welsh personalities (only Bishop Short and Sir Watkins Williams Wynn), he acquired a camera in 1863 – after overcoming his scruples, for photography was not considered 'respectable' at that time. In 1867 he opened his own shop called The Cambrian Gallery and subsequently he went all over Wales taking several thousand photographic plates, the majority of which are housed in the National Library of Wales, Aberystwyth, Cardiganshire.

INTRODUCTION

Wales is a country of contrasts: the land of princes, poets and pit ponies; bards and blast furnaces; mountain tips like Snowdon and coal tips of the mining areas. Giraldus Cambrensis (Gerald de Barri, the Norman-Welsh Archdeacon of Brecon), writing about 1188, says this of the people:

'No one of this nation ever begs, for the houses of all are common to all; and they consider liberality and hospitality amongst the first virtues. So much does hospitality here rejoice in communication, that it is neither offered nor requested by travellers, who, on entering any house, only deliver up their arms. Those who arrive in the morning are entertained till evening with the conversation of young women, and the music of the harp; for each house has its young women and harps allotted to this purpose.'

As in all the Celtic countries, the griddle (or bakestone in Wales) was, and still is, the utensil most used for the cooking of basic foods, using oatmeal as the predominant cereal. Indeed the pancake in various forms is found in Ireland, Scotland, Wales and Brittany. Similarly as the Welsh language is closely connected with the Breton, so is the food. The onion-sellers from Brittany can always make themselves understood in Wales, and together the two peoples have a love of spices, herbs, sea-food of all kinds and cheese in their traditional dishes. It is worth noting that the word 'Welsh' comes from the Saxon for foreigner, *Wealhas*, and the Celts of Flanders are called 'Walloons', a word which comes from the same root.

As Welsh is a living language I have used the Welsh title for a dish wherever possible. Welsh rarebit is known all over the English-speaking world, but it is not often realized that *Sauce Bretonne* (in addition to the many other similar dishes noted in the book) used with eggs, fish, veal and poultry in Brittany makes use of the leek and is identical to Welsh methods of serving such foods.

Happily, I am no stranger to this strange and beautiful country, for my maternal great-aunt married a Welshman, my mother spent many years of her youth there, and at a very early age I saw my first Roman amphitheatre at Caerleon: the words of Geoffrey of Monmouth are a reality to me, more so than the endless verses of *Le Morte d'Arthur* I was made to recite in the evenings:

'On one side, the city was washed by that noble river, so that Kings and Princesses from the countries beyond the seas might have the convenience of sailing up it. On the other side, the beauties of the meadows and groves, and the magnificence of the royal palaces with gilded roofs that adorned it, made it even rival the grandeurs of Rome.'

These words, together with the smell of spices; the softness of goose-feather beds; the feel of a Welsh blanket around my ears; the vital warmth of a black-and-white sheepdog called Gelert, named after the hound of Llewelyn the Great, comprise my childhood memories of Wales.

But insofar as any book is written for a reason, this one is for the 'Friends of my Youth', the bards, writers, poets, musicians and painters of my generation; Thomas, Watkins, Jones, Richards, Powys, Price-Jones and Williams are names known throughout the world.

Deilginis,   Dalkey,
Baile Atha Cliath.   Dublin.

Theodora FitzGibbon, 1971.

SGADAN ABERGWAUN

Fishguard (Abergwaun being the Welsh for Fishguard, i.e. Aber, *river mouth,* Gwaun, *the name of the local river) Herrings are of exceptional quality and used in many unusual ways.*

8 medium-size filleted herrings
1 large peeled, cored and sliced apple
2 lb. peeled and sliced potatoes
1 large peeled and sliced onion
1 heaped teaspoon made mustard

1 teaspoon chopped sage
1 level tablespoon butter or margarine
salt and pepper to taste
boiling water

Lay the fillets of fish flat, sprinkle with salt and pepper, and paint over a little of the mustard on each, then roll up the fillets. Lightly grease an ovenproof dish and line it with half the sliced potatoes, then layer it with the sliced apple, then onion and finally the herring rolls. Sprinkle with chopped sage and season again. Cover with the remaining potatoes, and half fill the dish with boiling water. Put the rest of the butter on top in small pieces, cover and bake in a moderate oven (350° F.) for 45 minutes. Remove the lid, and allow the top to brown for a further $\frac{1}{2}$ hour.

This recipe can also be used with mackerel fillets, anchovies, pilchards, John Dory, or tuna fish, and half cider and half water can be used if liked.

Serves 4–6.

BARA CEIRCH

Oatcakes, Traditional. They were always eaten on May-day eve, around the Beltane bonfire.

Bara is Welsh for 'bread', and there are many traditional kinds of bread made in Wales, all of high quality (see page 90). Oatcakes still survive in many parts of the country, and generally speaking they are thinner than the Scottish variety. They always used to be baked on a flat piece of iron, sometimes with a handle so that it could be hung, sometimes made with three or four legs so that it stood over the heat. This is called a bakestone in English : in the west of Wales it is Llechfaen : *in the Rhondda, and Brecon, a* maen, *and in the north it can be called* gradell, *cognate with the old Gaelic word* greadeal. *A common word used all over Wales is* planc. *The mixture was always flattened by the palm of the hand on a board known as* pren peilliad. *Once made it is customary to leave them to harden in a warm place, traditionally a* diogyn *(a sluggard) in front of the fire. It is best not to make too many at a time; cook several, and whilst they are doing, press out some more. A heavy frying pan can be used if no bakestone or equivalent is available.*

'*They had smoked and dried goat hams and bacon; with bara geirch [sic] and buttermilk or whey to drink.' Tour in Wales, 1798.*

8 oz. (2 cups) fine oatmeal
2 teaspoons lard
2 teaspoons butter or margarine
½ tablespoon sugar
pinch of salt
1½ gills (¾ cup) hot water (90° F. approx.)

FOR THE GLAZE
1 egg beaten with 1 tablespoon milk and 1 teaspoon sugar

Melt the butter and lard in the water with the sugar and salt and whilst still hot add to the oatmeal, kneading it well to a soft dough. Sprinkle oatmeal fairly thickly onto a board and put the dough on it, rolling it in the oatmeal. Break off small balls one at a time and flatten them on the board with the palm of the hand, about ⅛ in. thick, to the required size (about 3 in. across is easiest). Place onto a moderately hot bakestone: there is no need to grease it provided there is sufficient oatmeal on the surface to stop it sticking; paint on the glaze lightly to give the oatcakes a shiny surface when cooked. In the old days my great-aunt always kept some goose feathers tied together near by, and these were used to brush off any excess oatmeal from the bakestone. Bake the oatcakes (about 3 to 4 at a time depending on the size of both cakes and bakestone) for about 7 minutes on one side. Leave to harden in a warm place, or toast the *second* side under a slow grill or broiler when needed. As the mixture hardens quite quickly if the room is not warm, it is sometimes advisable to make half the above quantity first, and then mix the remainder when the first batch have been made. They keep for months in a tin.

Makes about 12 oatcakes.

A foolproof method, although not traditional, is to use 6 oz. (1½ cups) oatmeal and 2 oz. (½ cup) flour. This mixture is easier to handle, the cakes do not break so easily, and they can be pressed much thinner. Serve with butter, honey, or eat them with laverbread (see page 88), cheese, fish, etc., and drink buttermilk with them.

Post Office, St David's, Pembrokeshire, c. 1870; photographer, John Thomas. Cais ddoeth yn ei dyddyn – *Seek the wise in his cottage*

TEISEN LAP

Teisen *means 'cake' and* lap, *a plate, so that this is a Plate Cake. They are traditionally made all over Wales.*

8 oz. (2 cups) flour
4 oz. (½ cup) butter
1 heaped tablespoon lard
1 heaped teaspoon baking powder
½ teaspoon grated nutmeg
4 oz. (½ cup) sugar

4 oz. (1 cup) mixed currants and
seedless raisins or sultanas
2 eggs, well beaten
approx. ¼ pint (½ cup) cream,
milk or buttermilk

Rub the fat into the flour and add the dry ingredients. Mix in the well-beaten eggs, and add gradually enough cream or milk to make a fairly soft mixture. Beat well, and either grease a shallow tin or plate and put the mixture in, or roll out to 1-in. thickness, on a floured table, cut into rounds and cook on a moderate bakestone or hotplate for about 15 minutes each side. If cooking in the shallow tin or plate, cook in a moderate oven (350° F.) for 20 minutes then lower the heat to 275° F. for about 40 minutes. Test with a skewer before removing from the oven, and turn out to cool on a wire rack.

A miner's stove and hearth, The Triangle, Merthyr Tydfil, Glamorgan, c. 1905

BRAISED GAME BIRDS

Montgomeryshire abounds in game of many kinds, and is also known for the excellence of its fish, Lake Vyrnwy providing some of the best fishing in Wales. The River Dovey is noted for its salmon, and the tributaries contain excellent trout. At Machynlleth seasonal fairs are still held, the 'stondings' being set around the trees in the roadway.

Recipe from the Lake Vyrnwy Hotel, for using any aged game bird: grouse, pheasant, partridge or pigeon, or a combination of several of them.

2 pheasant or equivalent in other birds, and the giblets	1 large onion
	2 large carrots
2 oz. (2 tablespoons) butter or oil	2 turnips
1 tablespoon flour	2 leeks (if available)
¼ bottle red wine	1 parsnip
salt and pepper	sprig of parsley, thyme
1 bayleaf	½ teaspoon chopped rosemary
water	

Take a heavy-bottomed stewpan and on the bottom make a bed about 4–5 in. deep of the peeled and coarsely cut root vegetables, and game giblets, herbs and seasonings. Add water almost to cover the vegetable bed, and let it simmer gently. Meanwhile heat the butter and lightly fry the birds, then set them on top of the vegetables but retain the butter. Cover with foil and a tight lid, and simmer gently for 2 hours, or until the birds are tender. The birds, being out of the liquor, never break up, for they steam in the aromatic stock. When cooked, heat up the butter they were cooked in and mix in the flour, then pour over ½ pint (1 cup) of the game stock, and the red wine. Reduce rapidly on top of the stove, and serve over the carved portions of game. This is a simple recipe which, however, preserves all the fine flavour and succulence of the birds.

Serves 6–8.

'He enjoyed our Welsh woodcock shooting exceedingly and wore a red hat-band by way of being seen, as security.' Mrs John Henry Vivian's diary, 1822, about Sir Humphry Davy.

Shooting party, Montgomeryshire, c. 1885; photographer, John Thomas

BARA SINSIR

Welsh Gingerbread, traditionally made at many old Welsh fairs. In fact it is rather a misnomer, for it has no ginger in it, but tastes just as though it had!

6 oz. (½ cup) black treacle (molasses)
¼ pint (½ cup) milk
1 level teaspoon bicarbonate of soda
1 level teaspoon cream of tartar

12 oz. (3 cups) plain flour
4 oz. (½ cup) butter or margarine
6 oz. (¾ cup) demerara (soft brown) sugar
2 oz. (½ cup) chopped mixed peel

Warm the milk and treacle together, then sift the flour with the bicarbonate of soda and the cream of tartar. Rub the butter into this until it is like fine breadcrumbs, mix in the sugar and peel, and finally stir in the milk and molasses. Mix very thoroughly, then grease and line a tin about 8 in. long and 3 in. wide and pour in the mixture. Bake in a slow to moderate oven (approx. 300° F.) for about 1½ hours, or until a skewer can be inserted and come out clean. If liked, halved almonds and slices of crystallized ginger can be put on top half way through cooking time.

Butcher's and baker's boys gossiping, Tenby, Pembrokeshire, 1901

TATWS RHOST – HOT-POT

The waterways of Merioneth contain not only gold, for in Lake Bala there lives a mysterious fish the Welsh call Gwyniad. It is a species of fresh-water Whitefish (Coregonus lavaretus) *and highly prized when caught, both for food and for its rarity. It is sometimes cast up on the shore after storms. Related species are found only in certain lakes, such as the Pollan in Lough Derg, Shannon, Ireland; the Schelly in the Lake District of England, and the Vendace found in Lochmaben, Scotland. The Sig found in some Siberian lakes is a close relative. It is excellent to eat and can be fried, grilled or baked.*

1½ lb. potatoes
3 large onions, peeled and thinly sliced
1 lb. thickly sliced smoked bacon or raw ham
2 tablespoons chopped parsley
salt and pepper
½ pint (1 cup) water, stock, or cider

Peel and slice the potatoes thickly, but slice the onions thinly and leave the bacon rashers whole, but with the rinds trimmed off. In a fireproof dish start with a layer of potatoes at the bottom then add bacon, parsley and finally onion, all seasoned well. Repeat this until it is all used up, finishing with a layer of potato. Pour over the stock, put a sheet of greased foil on top, then the lid and cook slowly in a slow oven (250° F.) for about 2 hours. Remove the lid and foil for the last 20 minutes to allow the top to brown.

Serves 4.

It goes very well with Welsh beer or cider.

Panning for gold in the valley of the River Mawddach, Merioneth, 1899

P WDIN REIS GRIFFITHS

It was on just such a sturdy, resolute Welsh pony that I took my first fall, at the age of seven, on a farm near Trawsfynydd. Pollyanna, for that was her name, had been hired for my holiday, and the first time I opened the gate to hack across country she made straight for, as the crow flies, her own home, across hedges and ditches. An humiliating experience for an Irish girl, later ameliorated by the superb rice pudding which Mrs Griffiths had made for dinner. Welsh rice puddings are in a category of their own: creamy, spicy and delicious.

Mrs Griffiths's Rice Pudding

2 oz. ($\frac{1}{4}$ cup) rice
$\frac{1}{2}$ pint (1 cup) water
2 oz. ($\frac{1}{4}$ cup) demerara (soft brown) sugar
1 heaped tablespoon butter
a good pinch grated nutmeg

1 pint (2 cups) milk
1 bayleaf
2 small separated eggs or 1 large
1 heaped tablespoon caster (extra fine) sugar

Simmer the rice in the water for about 10 minutes then drain the liquid off. To the rice add all the other ingredients except the eggs and caster sugar, and either cook in a double boiler on top of the stove or in a very moderate oven (300° F.) for about $1\frac{1}{2}$ hours. Remove from the heat and stir in the beaten egg-yolks, then return to the oven for a further $\frac{1}{2}$ hour. Meanwhile beat the egg-whites until stiff with the caster sugar and, just before serving, fold this into the rice pudding. If serving hot, put it back into a cool oven just to set the whites, but it is also very good served cold later on. Jam, honey, or a compôte of oranges is often served with this rice dish.

Serves 4–6.

Rice pudding is almost traditional Sunday fare served after roast lamb or mutton. *See* page 100.

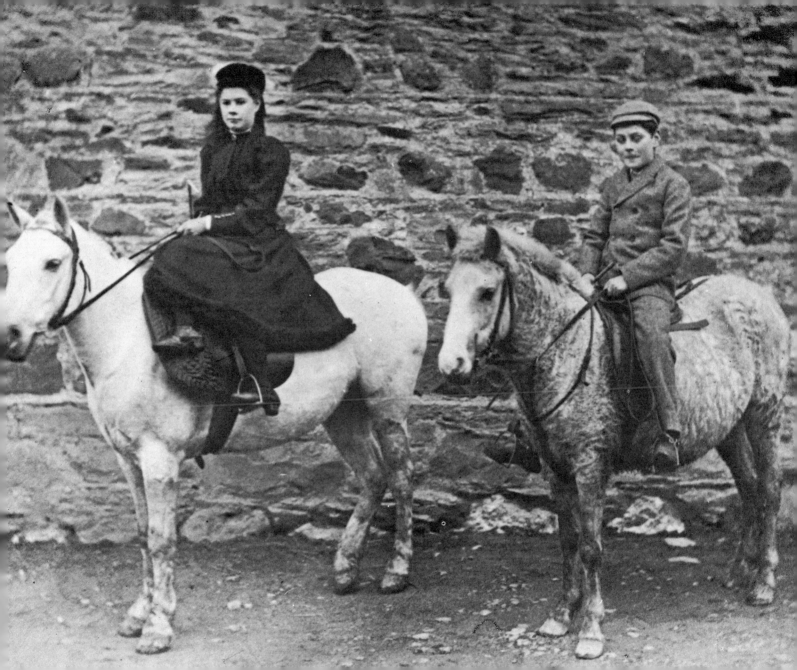

CREGYN GLEISION – MUSSELS

Swansea has long been known for the excellence of its sea-food; Swansea Market is still thriving and every day fresh supplies of cockles, mussels, laverbread, as well as a great variety of fish are to be found there. It is also a general market where the freshest of foods are sold.

MUSSEL STEW

60–80 mussels, about 3 quarts
½ pint (1 cup) water
2 tablespoons oil or butter
1 clove crushed garlic (wild garlic called *rames* has always been plentiful in the Swansea district)
4 tablespoons sherry
6 small finely chopped mushrooms

1 large finely sliced onion
3 oz. approx. (1 cup) fine, fresh white breadcrumbs
2 teaspoons lemon juice
2 tablespoons chopped parsley
salt and white pepper
1 egg-yolk beaten with 4 tablespoons light cream

Well wash and scrub the mussels in cold running water to remove all traces of grit, sand, barnacles etc. Discard any that are open already. Put them into a large saucepan with the water, cover and cook on a gentle heat for about 5 minutes or until all the shells are open. Strain off the liquid and reserve. Then break off one side of the mussel-shell (retaining any juices that escape) and remove the beards. Heat up the oil or butter and very lightly fry the onion, garlic and finally the mushrooms, and drain off any excess oil. Add the breadcrumbs, lemon juice, liquid from the mussels, parsley and sherry, and season to taste. Bring just up to boiling point then simmer gently for about 5 minutes. Finally add the egg-yolk and cream beaten together, stir well, then put in the mussels, and heat up. At no time should the sauce reboil once the egg-yolk and cream are added.

Serves 4–6.

MUSSEL SOUP

If a more soup-like dish is required cook the mussels in 1 pint (2 cups) water, omit the breadcrumbs and remove both shells from the mussels, otherwise proceed as above. Serve with hot bread spread with garlic butter.

Cockles, clams or scallops can be used in place of mussels for the above dishes.

BRITHYLL Â CHIG MOCH – TROUT WITH BACON

This exceptional mountain railway at Tan-y-bwlch and Minffordd was built in 1836 to run between Blaenau Ffestiniog and Portmadoc. This station was closed in 1946, but by popular demand has been reopened. The superb mountains around conceal slate quarries, but there are also many lakes, notably Llyn y Morynion (which is Crown property, but fishing rights are allowed for payment) stocked with excellent trout.

This is a well known Welsh method of cooking trout which is exactly the same as the French *Truites au lard*. It is possibly a direct Celtic link with Brittany.

6 trout	1 tablespoon chopped parsley
12 thin rashers of smoked bacon, half lean, half fat	salt and pepper

Split and clean the trout and remove the bones. Line a fireproof dish with half the bacon rashers, lay the trout on top, season well, and sprinkle the parsley over. Then cover with the remaining bacon rashers, and bake in a hot oven (400° F.) for 15–20 minutes.
  Serves 4–6.

Narrow-gauge railway, Tan-y-bwlch, Ffestiniog, Merioneth (built 1836), c. 1875

PWDIN ERYRI – SNOWDON PUDDING

Snowdon is the highest mountain in Wales, the central peak being 3,560 feet above sea-level. Surrounding the peak are the Llanberis pass, Aberglaslyn pass and the Rhyd-ddu pass. There are several lakes in the valleys rising up to these passes. The northern slopes carry the only mountain railway in Britain, which is of the rack-and-pinion, steam-driven variety perfected in Switzerland. It was first opened in 1896.

Snowdon Pudding (*eryri* means eagle's nest) used to be served at the hotel at the foot of the mountain about seventy years ago. It is a good steamed pudding served with an excellent wine sauce. Recipe from Alice Corbett, 1887.

4 oz. (1 cup) grated suet (butter or margarine can also be used but are not traditional)

4 oz. (2 cups firmly pressed down) white breadcrumbs

1 oz. (1 tablespoon) cornflour (cornstarch) or ground rice

pinch of salt

finely grated rind of 1 lemon

3 oz. (scant cup) lemon or orange marmalade

3 oz. (3 tablespoons) brown sugar

3 well-beaten eggs

3 tablespoons seedless raisins

a little butter

TO MAKE THE PUDDING

Take a pudding basin about 6 in. high and grease it well with the butter, then press as many of the seedless raisins onto the sides as it will take. Mix together the suet, breadcrumbs, cornflour and salt, then add the grated lemon rind, marmalade and sugar. Beat the eggs well and mix them in and any raisins that are left over. Spoon the mixture into the basin, taking care not to dislodge the raisins. Cover with foil tied down, and either steam the pudding or simmer it in a saucepan with boiling water to half-way up the basin for 50–60 minutes. See that the saucepan is topped up with water. Turn out onto a warmed plate and serve with the Wine Sauce, which you can make whilst the pudding is cooking.

SAWS GWIN – WINE SAUCE

2 oz. (2 tablespoons) sugar

½ lemon rind in one piece

2 tablespoons water

1 teaspoon cornflour (cornstarch)

1 tablespoon butter

¼ pint (½ cup) Madeira, sweet sherry, Marsala, red wine or home-made sweet wine, white or red

TO MAKE THE WINE SAUCE

Boil the sugar, lemon rind and water for 15 minutes then take out the rind. Mix the cornflour into the butter thoroughly and stir into the sugar mixture, then add the wine and let it simmer gently until the liquid has become syrupy, about 10 minutes. It should be served in a separate sauceboat, very hot.

Serves 4.

Ascending Mount Snowdon, Caernarvonshire, by pony and foot, from Llanberis, September 1907

CAWL LLYSIAU GARDD – GARDEN VEGETABLE SOUP

From *The First Principles of Good Cookery*, by Lady Llanover, 1867.

2 lettuce	2 medium onions
1 cucumber	4 oz. approx. (1 cup) old green
3 leeks (or green onions)	peas or peashells
1 stalk celery	4 oz. approx. (1 cup) fresh young
3 pints (6 cups) chicken stock	green peas
salt and pepper to taste	1 teaspoon each of basil and mint
½ lb. spinach	cream for garnish (optional)

Prepare all the vegetables for cooking, and slice up the onions, cucumber, leeks and celery. Put all ingredients except the young green peas, basil and mint into a large saucepan and cook gently for 1 hour. Sieve it well, or put through a vegetable mill and taste for seasoning. Put back into a saucepan, add the fresh green peas, basil and mint and cook gently for about 10 minutes until the peas are just tender. Serve with a spoonful of cream in each plate if liked.
Serves 4–6.

RHUBARB AND GOOSEBERRY JAM

From *The First Principles of Good Cookery*, by Lady Llanover, 1867.

This jam has a delicious flavour, strangely enough not unlike apricots. The elderflowers add a grape-like taste, but the jam is very good without them. It was given to Lady Llanover by Mrs Faulkener, of Tenby, South Wales, previously landlady of the White Lion Hotel there, when she was aged 93. Mrs Faulkener was born in 1774.

4 lb. chopped rhubarb	4 lb. unripe gooseberries
6 lb. (12 cups) sugar	6 heads of elderflowers (optional)
water to cover	

Top and tail the gooseberries and wipe the rhubarb before cutting it into pieces. Put into a large pan with the sugar and barely cover with water. Bring to the boil, then boil rapidly for about ½ hour, or until a little jam put onto a cold saucer 'wrinkles' up when cold. Just before it is ready plunge in the elderflowers and let them steep in the hot jam for 10 minutes, then remove them. Pour into warmed sterilized jars and seal as usual.
Makes about 12 lb. of jam.

Mrs Jones selling produce in Old Market Hall, c. 1904

WYAU SIR FÔN – ANGLESEY EGGS

Whether there is a traditional Welsh costume is open to question. Certainly it was not generally worn before the nineteenth century, unlike the Kinsale cloak of West Cork, or the goffered head-dresses of Brittany. Nevertheless the non-Welsh person likes to think of the tall hats and aprons as being typically Welsh, in much the same way as the kilt is connected with Scotland. Those interested in the subject will enjoy F. G. Payne's booklet, Welsh Peasant Costume, *obtainable from the Welsh Folk Museum, St Fagans, Glamorgan. The 'Tavern friend' is worth looking at no matter how authentic her costume is.*

Anglesey has an interesting Easter egg custom which survives today. It is called Clepian wyau *in Anglesey, to clap for eggs. This takes place on the Monday before Easter, and children go round asking for eggs, chanting, 'Clap, clap, gofyn ŵy, i hogia' bach ar y plwy' – 'Clap, clap, ask for an egg for little boys on the parish', at the same time making a clapping noise with wooden clappers.*

Anglesey eggs are very similiar to *Œufs à la Bretonne* served in Brittany.

6 medium-sized leeks (green onions can be used if leeks are not available)	8 hard-boiled eggs
	1 lb. (2 cups) hot mashed potato
	salt and pepper
2 tablespoons butter	1 tablespoon flour
2 oz. (⅔ cup) plus 2 tablespoons grated cheese	½ pint (1 cup) warm milk

Clean the leeks and chop them into pieces, then cook them in boiling salted water for 10 minutes. Strain very well, and add them to the hot mashed potato. Add half the butter, season to taste and beat until it is a pale green fluff. Arrange around the edge of an oval or round fireproof dish and keep warm. Then heat the other tablespoon of butter, stir in the flour and add the warmed milk, stirring well to avoid lumps. Put in the 2 oz. grated cheese and mix well. Cut up the eggs and put in the middle of the leek and potatoes and cover with the cheese sauce. Sprinkle the remaining cheese on top and put into a hot oven (400° F.) until the top is golden brown.

Serves 4.

APRICOCKE WINE

From a manuscript of Anne Wynne, later Madam Owen of Penrhos, Anglesey, 1675.

'Your fruit must be very ripe, then take to every gallon of boyling water a pound and a half of good powder sugar; paire your apricockes and mashe them and ye peele along with them, by sure to take ye stones out; your sugar must be boyled with the watter till the rawness of the watter be boyled, then have in readiness your apricockes in an earthen vessell, so pour the hott Liquor upon them and let them lye 2 days sturring them twice a day, then straine them through a haire sieve, barrill it up for a fortnight, then bottle it with a lump of sugar in each bottle.'

Tavern Friend, Beaumaris, Anglesey, c. 1865; photographer, John Thomas

PASTEIOD CENNIN – LEEK PASTIES OR TURNOVERS

Both the leek and the daffodil are national emblems of Wales and both can be worn on St David's Day (March 1st), the feast of the patron saint of Wales. Various theories have been advanced as to why these plants were chosen, one being that the green and white colours of Valois were in Henry Tudor's coat-of-arms. When he was in exile his followers recognized one another by producing any flower or vegetable which showed a green stem going to white at the root end. As both these plants were common all over Wales it is easy to see why they were chosen.

Leek Pasties make ideal picnic fare, for they are enclosed in pastry and no knives and forks are needed. They are a Welsh speciality, but if leeks are not available the pasties are extremely good made with scallions or young onion tops, mixed with a little chopped bacon. Bacon is sometimes added to leek pasties but the flavour is very pure and good without it. Serve with green salad.

	FOR THE PASTRY
12 large leeks (the white part only)	1 lb. (4 cups) flour
1 teaspoon lemon juice	8 oz. (1 cup) lard, butter or margarine
1 teaspoon sugar	1 teaspoon baking powder (unless using self-raising flour)
a pinch of salt	a pinch of salt
a little cream (optional)	¼ pint (½ cup) cold water approx.
1 egg-yolk	

If using bacon as well allow ½ lb. mixed fat and lean rashers.

Clean and trim the leeks well, for they can retain a lot of soil between the leaves; a sure way of cleaning them thoroughly is under running water. Trim the green ends then make a cross on that part. Stand them in a deep jug of cold water, green end down, and leave for several hours. Cut the white part into 1-in. pieces and cook them in salted boiling water to which the sugar and lemon juice have been added, for not more than 5 minutes. Then drain well and let them cool. Make the pastry by rubbing the fat into the flour and salt, then add the water slowly, mixing well all the time. Turn out onto a floured board and roll out to a thickness of about ½ in. then cut into oblongs about 6 in. long and 4 in. wide; this amount should make about twelve. Allow one large leek for each pasty, laying it along the middle of the pastry. If using cream add a very little to each pasty just to moisten it, sprinkle with salt, then wet the edges with water and draw up the sides, pressing well to keep the edges together. Brush over with beaten egg-yolk and bake for 15–20 minutes in a hot oven (400° F.).

Serves about 6.

See also Leek Tart, page 82.

GWLYBWR HUFEN – CREAM SALAD DRESSING

Adapted from a Radnorshire farmhouse recipe by Mr Tasker Davies.

¼ pint (½ cup) fresh cream	2 tablespoons white wine vinegar
1 teaspoon soft brown sugar (or more to taste)	a squeeze of lemon
a little freshly ground black pepper	salt to taste

Mix the sugar, lemon juice and wine vinegar together well, then stir in the cream. Add salt and pepper to taste after mixing well.

Picnic in the Gower Peninsula, 1841; photographer, Henry H. Vivian

KATT PIE

Minsterley, in the English border county of Salop, was a great centre for the mining of lead and barytes in the last century. Fairs were general all over the country from the thirteenth century, but they were in no way the fun-fairs of today. Generally speaking they were large markets held on a Saint's Day where people came to trade as well as to enjoy themselves. Every fair had its own district and in many places the people could sell their animals and produce only at these fairs, which took place at all times of the year except deep winter. Clogs, shoes, clothes as well as food were on sale, and ballad singers usually visited. Fairs were enjoyed by people of all ages; cakes (see Cacs Ffair Llanddarog, page 59), Treacle Toffee (page 118) and especially mutton pies or pasties were eaten. Many of these large fairs took place in November; some were hiring fairs (called mop fairs) where men and women servants were hired. St Martin's Fair, Trevine, Pembrokeshire, went on until early this century, and small mutton pies were a speciality. Templeton Fair, Pembrokeshire (November 12th), specialized in Katt Pie for over two hundred years.

Traditional

FOR THE CRUST
1 lb. flour
8 oz. grated suet
½ teaspoon salt
1½ gills (¾ cup) boiling water

FOR THE FILLING
1 lb. lean minced mutton or lamb
8 oz. (1 cup) currants
6 oz. (½ cup) brown sugar
salt and pepper
a little milk or beaten egg

Serves 4.

TO MAKE THE PASTRY

Boil the suet in the water for 5 minutes, then stir in the flour mixed with the salt and mix very thoroughly until the mixture leaves the sides. Turn out quickly onto a thickly floured board and roll out to a thickness of just under ½ in. This should be done quickly before the suet hardens. When cool, cut into circles, or more easily into two large circles, and place on a greased tin the correct size. Arrange the filling in layers: currants, sugar and mutton, seasoned to taste. Moisten with water around the edges and put on the lid, pressing down tightly to keep the filling in. Make a small incision on top to let the air escape, brush over with milk or egg and bake in a moderate oven for about 30–40 minutes. Eat warm.

Nowadays when suet pastry is not often used, this pie can be made either with short-crust pastry (see page 63), or butter or margarine can be substituted for the suet in the above recipe. Personally I prefer this pie made in a deep pie dish rather than in individual small ones, for the fruit, sugar and meat amalgamate in a delicious manner.

The Miners' Arms, Minsterley Fair, c. 1890; photographer, John Thomas

FAGOTS – FAGGOTS

Faggots are exactly the same as the French crépine *or* crépinettes *and yet another link with Brittany, for they are a speciality of Wales, although a similar dish called 'savoury ducks' is found in the north of England and I suspect that these were a Welsh inheritance. As in France, they were always made around pig-killing time, usually from not only the liver but also other intestines, and traditionally they were wrapped in the pig's flead – that is, the thin, lacy membrane marbled with fat, from the pig's inside. They are still made daily in Wales, and can be found in many supermarkets. Both faggots and various pasties were eaten a lot in Wales, especially by miners, quarry and furnace workers, for they were easy to transport, could be made at least the day before and provided valuable protein needed for such strenuous work. They are extremely good, much enjoyed by all ages.*

Put the finely minced liver and onions into a large bowl, then add the breadcrumbs or oatmeal and all the other ingredients and mix very thoroughly. Grease a large meat tin and put the mixture in, and if possible cover with a sheet of pork flead, but if not available use greased foil. Cook in a slow to moderate oven (about 250° F.) for 40–60 minutes, but after 20 minutes take from the oven and mark into squares with a knife. Fifteen minutes before it is ready remove the foil (not the flead if using it) to let the tops get brown. Leave in the tin to get cold and when serving break them apart. They can be eaten cold with salad, and apple-sauce, or if wanted hot, pour over about $\frac{1}{2}$ pint (1 cup generous) of good stock to make a gravy, and re-heat.

2 lb. pigs' liver minced (as this is now difficult to get, calves' or lambs' liver can also be used)

4 oz. (2 cups) breadcrumbs *or* 4 oz. (1 cup) oatmeal

4 oz. (1 cup) grated suet *or* 4 oz. ($\frac{1}{2}$ cup) butter or margarine

2 large onions, minced

a pinch of nutmeg or mace, about $\frac{1}{2}$ teaspoon

2 teaspoons chopped sage (bog myrtle was used originally)

1 teaspoon chopped thyme

2 teaspoons salt

$\frac{1}{2}$ teaspoon black pepper

Serves 4–6.

Chwarel y Llechwedd (Llechwedd Slate Quarry), Cardiganshire, c. 1900

E OG – SALMON

'*The noble river Teivi* [sic] *flows here, and abounds with the finest salmon, more than any other river in Wales; it has a productive fishery near Cilgerran, which is situated on the summit of a rock, at a place called Canarch Mawr* [Kenarth], *the ancient residence of St Ludoc, where the river, falling from a great height, forms a cataract, which the salmon ascend, by leaping from the bottom to the top of a rock, which is about the height of the longest spear, and would appear wonderful, were it not the nature of that species of fish to leap: hence they have received the name of salmon, from* salio.'
Giraldus Cambrensis (Gerald the Welshman), Itinerary Through Wales, c. 1188.

The coracle is still in use in Wales for salmon fishing and also for dipping and washing sheep. It is a very light boat which used to be made from horse or ox hide stretched over osiers, but nowadays tar-coated canvas is used. It was formerly also in use in Ireland, but since the thirties has been replaced by the larger curragh. *This type of boat was in use when Julius Caesar invaded Britain. He commented on it and employed it in his Spanish campaign. Coracle fishing is done by two men, each in his coracle, one hand holding the net whilst the other uses the paddle. When the fish is caught the net is hauled up until the two coracles meet and the fish is taken from the net.*

Salmon should be cooked simply for it has a delicious flavour without the use of elaborate forms of cooking. A whole fish can be rubbed with butter and lemon, wrapped in double foil and either baked in a moderate oven (350° F.) for 15 minutes to the pound, or gently poached in boiling salted water with a dash of vinegar or lemon juice for the same length of time. If serving it cold, leave it in the water until you want it, then drain carefully, remove the skin and set it on a handsome dish. Serve with mayonnaise; or whipped cream or yoghurt with grated cucumber in it.

Small cuts, or steaks, can also be poached or grilled: in the latter case brush them over with oil first, and do not have the grill too hot, for if thick the fish would burn before being cooked through. Serve with a nut of butter worked with a little lemon juice and fresh, chopped parsley.

SAWS EOG TEIFI

A Teifi sauce for cooking a tail-end of salmon or for other small amounts.

2 lb. salmon	8 oz. (1 cup) melted butter
¼ pint (½ cup) Port	1 teaspoon mushroom ketchup
1 anchovy fillet	salmon stock

Wash the salmon well, remove all skin, bones etc., and cut it into chunks. Boil up the trimmings in ½ pint (1 cup) water well seasoned for ½ hour, then strain it and reserve the liquid. It should have boiled down considerably, but have a good strong flavour. Mash up the anchovy and add the salmon and all the other ingredients, and put into a fireproof dish. Cover and bake in a hot oven (400° F.) and bake for about 40 minutes.

Serves 4.
See also page 99.

Coracle Fishermen, Cardigan (Aberteifi), c. 1880

CIG OEN, CIG DAFAD – LAMB OR MUTTON

The supper was an excellent one too . . . the tea service was extremely plain . . . but the bread and the mutton chops, and the butter and even the tea, were such as Mrs Powell's china was never privileged to bear.
Susan Warner's description of a Welsh farmhouse, c. 1850.
The small Welsh sheep has a sweetness and succulence accepted everywhere as being extremely fine. The herds range freely over the hills where the wild thyme grows which gives them a characteristic flavour. The joints are very small, a leg being perhaps not more than 4 lb. on a full-grown animal. Likewise the chops are sometimes no longer than 4 inches, but excellently tender and juicy.

GOLWYTHAU CIG DAFAD – MUTTON OR LAMB CHOPS

2–3 chops per person if small; they should be dusted with black pepper, sprinkled with chopped thyme and grilled quickly under a hot grill for about 5 minutes each side. In Wales they are sometimes served with a lump of butter worked with freshly chopped mint and a little rowanberry jelly.

SAWS CRIAFOL, or Rowanberry Sauce

3 lb. rowan berries	2 large, chopped apples
sugar	water

Put the berries and chopped apples (no need to peel or core them) into a large saucepan, cover with water and boil for 40 minutes. Drain through muslin and let it drip overnight. Then boil up the liquid allowing 1 lb. sugar for every pint of juice. Boil fairly fast for about 1 hour. Bottle and seal as for jam. Makes about 5 lb. jelly.

GOLWYTHAU CIG OEN Â PHYS – LAMB CHOPS WITH PEAS

8 small lean chops	salt and pepper
chopped mint, about 1 tablespoon	2 lb. green peas
1 level tablespoon cornflour	1 pint (2 cups) water
(cornstarch)	1 teaspoon sugar

Trim the chops of fat, and dust them with black pepper, then boil up the water with the sugar and just a pinch of salt. When boiling add the shelled peas and cook for 5 minutes, strain, but reserve the liquid. Put the peas in the bottom of a casserole and sprinkle over the chopped mint. Then cream the cornflour with 2 tablespoons of water, heat up the pea stock and stir it in, mixing well until it is quite smooth. Pre-heat the grill, and also the oven to 350° F. and quickly sear the chops on both sides. Pour the pea stock over the peas in the casserole, then lay the chops on top and put, uncovered, into the oven for 20 minutes. Serve with very finely puréed potatoes.
Serves 4.

St Mary Street, Cardiff, 1891 ; photographer, Collings

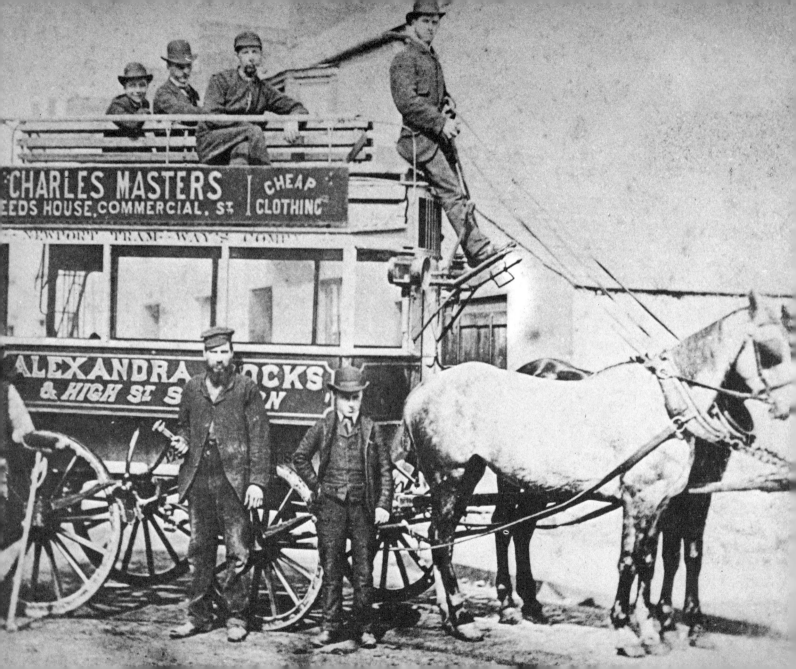

CAWL CYMREIG - WELSH CAWL

Cawl pronounced 'cowl', is Welsh for broth or soup. Like all traditional country soups the ingredients are governed by what is to hand or in season. It appears from early Welsh manuscripts that originally the main meat used was bacon, or even kid, for as with Irish Stew no cottager would dream of using valuable lamb or mutton for soups. Nowadays, however, mutton or lamb best end of neck chops are most generally used, which make it into a delicious soup-stew.

'Cystal yfed o'r cawl â bwyta'r cig' – 'It is as good to drink the broth as to eat the meat': from a collection of proverbs attributed to Cattwg Ddoeth (Cattwg the Wise).

Cawl should be started the day before so that any fat can be skimmed off and all the flavours amalgamate.

2–3 lb. best end of neck cutlets	2 tablespoons chopped parsley
1 large sliced onion	6 small potatoes
3 leeks	salt and pepper
2 medium sliced carrots	4 pints (8 cups) water
1 medium parsnip	If in season cabbage, celery, etc.,
1 small swede turnip *or* 2 white turnips	can all be used

Trim the meat of fat so far as possible, cover with cold water, add salt and pepper, bring to the boil, and simmer slowly for 1 hour, then leave it to get cold and skim off all the fat. Put in all the vegetables except 1 leek, the potatoes and half the parsley, cover and simmer very slowly for 1 hour, then add the potatoes cut in half and continue cooking for 20 minutes. Then add the remainder of the parsley, taste for seasoning, and finely chop the remaining leek (green and white part) on top. Let it cook for not more than 5 minutes and serve. Some families treat it as a French *pot-au-feu* – that is, they serve the clear broth first, then the meat and vegetables as a second course. Traditionally Cawl was eaten in wooden bowls with wooden spoons so that there was no fear of burning the mouth.

Serves 4–6.

Horse Tram, Newport, Monmouthshire, c. 1885

Cocos – COCKLES

The blind fisherman lived at 12 Fleet Street, Swansea, and walked the five miles there and back to Mumbles daily. It is said he was an expert fisherman, knew where to find the fish and never once lost a net, although he was blind from birth.

Swansea is still a great cockle-eating area and they can be found daily in Swansea Market. They are served in several ways: in pies (see page 77), soups (see page 15), or simply plainly boiled, shelled, with brown bread and butter and a dash of vinegar or lemon.

Cockles are the same family (Cardium) as clams and there are over two hundred varieties. It is difficult to tell a cockle from a small clam, for they are both small bivalves with radial shell markings. Many cockles are exported daily to the Continent for use as clams. In Portugal they are served as a sauce with pork, which is one of the most delicious of Portuguese dishes. This Celtic method is also used in Wales, and Stone Age caves near Llandudno produced remains of oxen, bear and pigs alongside cockle shells, when excavated by Thomas Kendrick in 1879. The middens (moitas) of the lower valley of the Tagus river, Portugal, revealed similar finds. The Mesolithic peoples lived near rivers or on the coast: shellfish, together with various meats, constituted their main diet, and a characteristic implement found was a pick for prising shellfish from the rocks.

TEISEN GOCOS – COCKLE CAKES

6 dozen cockles (or clams), about 4 quarts
a little oatmeal
deep oil for cooking

FOR THE BATTER
8 oz. (2 cups) flour
2 tablespoons oil
1 separated egg
salt
½ pint (1 cup) tepid water

Stand the cockles in slightly salted water sprinkled with oatmeal for several hours, or overnight. Drain, then scrub them well to get rid of sand and grit. Put into a large saucepan with salted or sea-water to cover, bring to the boil for about 3 minutes or until they are open. Do not continue cooking once the shells open for it can make them rubbery. Leave until cool enough to handle, and meanwhile make the batter.

TO MAKE THE BATTER
Put the flour into a basin, add the salt and the oil, then stir in the beaten egg-yolk and the water. Beat with a beater until smooth, and do not be alarmed if the batter seems thick, for that is as it should be. Leave in a cool place to let the air in. Then remove the cockles from their shells with a sharp knife. Beat the egg-white until stiff, and fold into the batter. Heat up the oil until just under smoking, dip either one cockle or two together into the batter, drop into the hot oil with a spoon and fry until golden on all sides. Drain on absorbent paper. If lightly fried (until just coloured) they can be reheated without loss of taste or any lessening in the crispness of the batter. Serve with home-made wholemeal bread (page 90), and wedges of lemon.

Serves 4–6.

They are very good washed down with buttermilk, known as 'glaster' on Gower (see also page 77).

The Blind Fisherman of the Mumbles, aged 55, c. 1878

TEISEN FÊL – HONEY CAKE

'Brodyr pob cerddorion' – '*All musicians are brothers': from a collection of Welsh proverbs attributed to Cattwg Ddoeth (Cattwg the Wise).*

'*The Welch* [sic] *music is varied, expressive and pathetic.' J. W. Harding*, Sketches in North Wales, *1810.*

The Welsh love spiciness in their food. This cake is a good example, with honey and cinnamon giving it a distinctive and characteristic flavour. It makes a very elegant dessert, especially if served with rum-flavoured whipped cream.

8 oz. (2 cups) sifted flour
1 rounded teaspoon cinnamon
½ teaspoon bicarbonate of soda
4 oz. (½ cup) butter or margarine
4 oz. (½ cup) brown soft sugar
2 egg-yolks
3 egg-whites

4 oz. (½ cup) honey, warmed so that it is runny
1 tablespoon warmed honey
2 tablespoons caster (extra fine) sugar
a little milk (about 2 tablespoons) if eggs are small

Sieve together the flour, cinnamon and bicarbonate of soda. Separate the eggs, leaving 1 egg-white separate from the other 2. Cream the butter and sugar together, beat in the beaten egg-yolks and add the honey slowly, beating all the time. Stir in the flour mixture, and if it seems very stiff add the milk. Beat up the single egg-white until stiff and add to the mixture, folding it in gently. Grease an 8–9-in. tart tin and pour in the mixture, then bake in a hot oven (400° F.) for 20–25 minutes. Let it cool for 2 minutes, then remove from the tin and cool on a wire rack. Beat the remaining 2 egg-whites with the caster sugar, until thick. Brush the cake over with the tablespoon of warmed honey and roughly put the meringue mixture on top, so that it stands in points. Put back into a moderate oven (about 325° F.) for 10–15 minutes or until the meringue is set and very delicately golden on top.

This mixture can also be put into small patty pans if preferred, and the meringue on top omitted, in which case dredge the tops with fine sugar, either white or brown.

PRAWN OR SHRIMP PASTE

Recipe of my Great-Aunt Polly Mary, 1858–1953

1 lb. shelled cooked shrimps or prawns, but retain shells
12 oz. (1½ cups) butter
1 lb. filleted cod or fresh haddock

1 teaspoon anchovy essence or paste
3 filleted anchovies
a good pinch of mace
cayenne pepper

Shell the shrimps or prawns and put the washed shells on to boil in water to barely cover them, for ½ hour. Strain the liquid and then simmer the cod or haddock in it for 10 minutes. Lift out the fish and remove any skin, and reduce the fish stock until only about 1 tablespoon remains. Put the fish into it with the mace, anchovy essence or paste, anchovies and cayenne to taste, and pound to a very smooth paste. Now add all but 2 oz. (2 tablespoons) of the butter and beat again until smooth. Put in the prawns (cut up if large) and transfer to a saucepan, heat together, but do not cook, for about 3 minutes until it is all amalgamated, then press into a deep china dish. When cool melt the rest of the butter and pour over the top, chill until wanted for use. When cut it looks and tastes like a soft pink butter, studded profusely with prawns. We always had it for tea as a special treat, served with crisp toast. It makes an attractive buffet dish, and can be served on crisp lettuce.
Serves 6.

Shrimping in Gower, Glamorgan, c. 1841; photographer, Henry H. Vivian

GWYDD – GOOSE

Lord and Lady Llanover (who came from Monmouthshire) lived near Abergavenny and in the nineteenth century made the town a centre of a movement to revive Welsh culture. They inaugurated Cymreigyddion y Fenni, a literary society, and an annual Eisteddfod was held for over thirty years. The Eisteddfod programmes were bi-lingual, and covered all aspects of Welsh culture. Lady Llanover herself offered a prize of £5 in 1853 for the best collections of Welsh flannels, 'in real National checks and stripes with the Welsh names by which they are known . . . no specimens to be included which have not been well known for at least half a century'. She wrote several books and was also a painter of considerable merit.

Geese have always played a great part in Welsh rural life: not only are they the favourite Christmas or festive bird, but the feathers are used to make the down pillows, bed-coverings, and 'feather beds'—goose-down mattresses which are slept on. I still have one made by my great-aunt from the feathers of her own geese. The large wing-pinion was always used for sweeping the hearth, and smaller feathers brushed flour or oatmeal from the bakestone. Even today supermarkets in Wales can supply geese at all times of the year. An elaborate Christmas pie was made in Llansanffraid, Montgomeryshire, up to the turn of the century, consisting of boned goose stuffed with a whole tongue, and then roasted. The whole was wrapped in pastry lined with mincemeat, and then baked. This was served during the week of Christmas. In the early nineteenth century geese were first 'shod' by being made to walk through tar and then sand before being driven to market.

STUFFED ROAST GOOSE WITH SPICY APPLE SAUCE

1 10–12-lb. goose
goose giblets
4 tablespoons lard or oil
3 tablespoons Port or red wine

FOR THE SAUCE
½ lb. cooking apples
2 tablespoons sugar
1 teaspoon vinegar
2 tablespoons breadcrumbs
a pinch dry mustard
a pinch cinnamon

1 small chopped onion
¼ pint (½ cup) dark ale or stout

FOR THE STUFFING [1]
4 oz. (2 cups) fresh breadcrumbs
1 tablespoon chopped sage
1 medium peeled, cored and minced apple
1 medium sliced, chopped onion
1 separated egg
chopped liver of the bird
salt and pepper

Boil the giblets (but retain the liver for the stuffing) in salted water to cover for ½ hour. Mix all the stuffing ingredients together except the egg-white: whip that up stiffly and add last, then stuff the bird with this and secure. Put into a baking tin, pour the oil over, cover with foil and roast in a hot oven (400° F.) for 20 minutes to the pound, and after the first 20 minutes lower the heat to around 325° F. Baste about three or four times, and 15 minutes before it is ready, pour off the surplus fat, season well and add the giblet stock, and 3 tablespoons Port or red wine if available. Let it reduce on the top of the stove. Whilst the goose is cooking, cook the peeled and cored apples for the sauce with the onion, sugar and ale. When soft, stir in the breadcrumbs, vinegar, mustard, cinnamon and a little of the goose gravy. Simmer it all for 10 minutes and serve hot, with the bird.

Serves about 8.

[1] From *The First Principles of Good Cookery*, by Lady Llanover, 1867.

Monmouthshire Drag Club, at Abergavenny, April 1871

TORBWT WEDI EI FÔTSIO – POACHED TURBOT WITH GRANVILLE SAUCE

The forgotten Welsh poet who wrote a stirring poem in praise of Dinbych y-pysgod, *Tenby of the Fishes, certainly didn't envisage temperance hotels :*

'. . . *Louder the song of the bards at their mead*
Than the beat of the waves resounding below. . . .'

Granville Sauce can be served with almost any fish. It is particularly good with turbot, halibut, fresh haddock and other white fish. It comes from *The First Principles of Good Cookery*, by Lady Llanover, 1867.

4 thick cutlets turbot
1 medium onion, finely sliced
2 tablespoons chopped parsley
water to cover
salt and pepper

GRANVILLE SAUCE
1 chopped shallot or small onion
1 pounded anchovy
2 tablespoons sherry
2 teaspoons wine vinegar
6 peppercorns
a pinch of nutmeg and mace
1 tablespoon butter
1 tablespoon flour
6 tablespoons cream

Slice the onion very finely, and lay it on the bottom of a pan, then add the parsley, and put the turbot cutlets on top. Season well, pour water over barely to cover, lay some foil or a lid on top and poach very gently for 15–20 minutes depending on the thickness of the cutlets. Leave in the water until needed. Meanwhile make the sauce by simmering in a double boiler the first six ingredients until the shallot is soft. In another saucepan melt the butter, stir in the flour and mix until smooth, then add the first mixture, and simmer, stirring all the time. When smooth and cooked add the 6 tablespoons cream. Stir well, strain, or liquidize and serve warm with the strained fish.

Serves 4.

Temperance Hotel, Tenby, Pembrokeshire, c. *1900*

CACEN GNEIFIO – SHEARING CAKE

The hafod, *from Haf-bod,* is a summer residence, or a mountain farm, that in the valley being called a hendre. *When the snow melted and the first green appeared the workers would go up and open the summer dwelling, bringing with them dried oatcakes* (bara ceirch), *butter and cheese, on which, with curd dishes, they lived all summer, often using mountain herbs such as wild thyme or sweet gale to flavour the curd. Sometimes they might cook the weakling lamb or calf, making a stew with herbs and wild garlic, and afterwards they would enjoy wild bilberries and honey. The* hafod *usually had a large common-room and over it two rooms where the workers slept. When autumn came they drove the herds down to the lowland or* hendre *for the long winter. This method of farming is common to all mountainous countries. As communications became better these summer dwellings were enlarged, and the whole family would live in them.*

Shearing Cake is often made at shearing time.

1 lb. (4 cups) plain flour
1 rounded teaspoon baking powder
8 oz. (1 cup) butter
pinch of salt
12 oz. (1½ cups) brown soft sugar
1 tablespoon caraway seeds
grated rind and juice of 1 lemon
1 teaspoon grated nutmeg
½ pint (1 cup) milk
2 eggs

Rub the butter into the flour sifted with the baking powder, then add the sugar, lemon rind and juice, caraway seeds, nutmeg and a pinch of salt. Pour in the milk slowly, mixing well all the time, and finally add the well beaten eggs. Line a 9-in. cake tin with greased paper and pour in the cake mixture. Bake in a moderate oven (350° F.) for about 2 hours, lowering the heat to 300° F. after the first ½ hour. If the cake browns too quickly, cover the top with a piece of foil or greaseproof paper but remove it for the last ½ hour of cooking. When slightly cooled, turn out of the tin and place on a wire rack.

Shearing day at the Hafod, Ffermdy, Blaenrhondda, c. 1900

GWIN MWYAR DUON – BLACKBERRY WINE

(1) Place alternate layers of blackberries and sugar in wide-mouthed jars; allow to stand for three weeks but cover with a piece of sterilized muslin to keep out insects. Then strain off liquid and bottle, adding a small handful of raisins to each quart bottle. Cork lightly at first, but when no bubbles of gas are to be seen, cork tightly. This is simple to make and tastes not unlike a Port. Keep for at least three months before using, to enjoy it at its best.

(2) 12 lb. blackberries   8 lb. granulated sugar
    2 gallons (32 cups) boiling   1 oz. yeast
      water

Put the blackberries in a large earthenware or glass crock and pour the boiling water over. Cover with sterilized muslin and leave for 2 days, stirring well night and morning. Strain off the liquid and dissolve the sugar in it, then add the yeast spread on a small piece of toast or a lump of sugar, then stir again.

Transfer to a clean jar or crock, keeping some for topping up, and stand inside another pan to catch the overflow when fermentation begins. It will froth over the side, and should be filled up from the residue bottle. When it has stopped frothing, bottle and cork very loosely until no bubbles can be seen, then cork tightly. To ensure a clear wine re-bottle when a sediment occurs at the bottom. Keep for 4–6 months without drinking. This method can be used for making all home-made wines.

BLACKBERRY CURD

This is a very delicious preserve, resembling lemon curd, but made with blackberries.

2 lb. blackberries   ¾ lb. apples
juice of 2 lemons   8 oz. butter
water to cover   6 eggs
2½ lb. lump sugar

Simmer together the peeled and cored apples and the blackberries in water to cover until the fruit is soft. Pour through a sieve into a double boiler, add the juice of 2 lemons, the butter and the sugar. When it has all dissolved add the well-beaten eggs and continue cooking until the mixture thickens, stirring all the time. Pour into sterilized, warmed jars and seal as for jam.

Makes approximately 5–6 lb.

Blackberrying, Singleton Park, near Swansea, c. 1843; photographer, Henry H. Vivian

SWPER MAM – MOTHER'S SUPPER

A good, quick supper dish popular in Wales.

8 large bacon rashers or ham slices
2 medium peeled and finely chopped onions
4 oz. (1 cup generous) grated hard cheese such as Cheddar
pepper and a little salt depending on the taste of the bacon or ham

Put half the bacon in the bottom of a shallow fireproof dish then cover with the finely chopped onions, followed by the cheese, seasoning each layer with pepper. Put the remaining rashers on top, and cook in a moderate to hot oven (375° F.–400° F.) for ½ hour, or until the bacon is crisp. Traditionally this is served either with jacket-baked potatoes, or with a Welsh omelette.
Serves 3–4.

CREMPOG LAS

Welsh Omelette, which is more like a pancake.

8 oz. (2 cups) plain flour
2 eggs, separated
4 tablespoons milk
2 teaspoons chopped parsley
a pinch of grated mace or nutmeg
salt
a small amount of lard or grease to oil the pan

Put the flour into a basin, and add the salt, mace, and the beaten egg-yolks. Mix well with a fork then stir in the milk, beating so that it is smooth. Whip the egg-whites until stiff, add the chopped parsley and finally fold in the egg-whites well, seeing they mix into the batter at the bottom of the basin as well as the top. In Wales this would be fried in a large pan and then cut into 4 for serving, but if preferred 4 separate pancakes can be made. Very lightly grease a heavy pan, let it get very hot, then pour in the batter. When the underneath is golden, turn and cook the other side the same way. Spread with butter and serve with Swper Mam.
Serves 3–4.

Landore Court, Cardiff, Glamorgan, 1891

POTTED HERRINGS

Recipe from Mrs Todd, West Cross, Swansea, c. 1880

6 filleted herrings
1 bayleaf
a pinch of mace
water or fish stock

½ teaspoon anchovy essence or paste
pepper and grated nutmeg to taste
4 tablespoons melted butter

Put the filleted herrings in an ovenproof dish with the bayleaf and a pinch of mace, all barely covered with water or stock. Cover with foil and bake in a moderate oven (350° F.) for 20 minutes, then let them cool slightly. Lift out the fish, remove all skin and any small bones that may be adhering to the rib-cage. Pound them well, mixing in the anchovy essence, pepper and grated nutmeg to taste. Put into a jar or pot, pressing down very well, and when quite cold pour the melted butter over the top. Serve cold, with toast, or it is particularly delicious with yeasted oatcakes.

Serves 4–6.

CREMPOG GEIRCH – OATMEAL PANCAKES

Traditional

8 oz. (2 cups) white sifted flour
3 oz. (¾ cup) fine oatmeal
½ oz. yeast creamed with 1 teaspoon sugar and 2 tablespoons tepid milk

1 egg
a pinch of salt
½ pint (1 cup) warm milk approx.
a little grease for frying

Mix together the oatmeal, flour and salt, then stir in the yeast. Finally add the well-beaten egg, cover and leave to rise for ½ hour in a warm place. Punch down, and if the mixture seems very thick, thin it down with the warm milk. The consistency should be a smooth batter that drops from a spoon, not too thin, so add the milk gradually until this is obtained. Cover again and leave to rise for ½ hour. Lightly oil a heavy pan as for a pancake, and drop the mixture in by a tablespoon at a time. (It is better to do them singly if you are not accustomed to making them.) Turn over and cook the other side, and if they are to be eaten at once, spread with butter. They will keep very well in a tin and can be re-heated either under a slow grill or in a low oven. Excellent with bacon, or with jam, honey, etc.

Makes about 20 oatcakes.

Fishermen's cottages, the Harbour, Tenby, Pembrokeshire, c. 1890

DIOD SINSIR – GINGER BEER

The arduous, stifling atmosphere of a tinplate works such as Cwmfelin created a regular thirst amongst its workers and considerable quantities of liquid refreshment were consumed. Some men favoured cold or hot tea, mineral waters etc., while others resorted to somewhat stronger beverages after working hours in nearby public houses. The consumption of ginger beer was another popular drink with many of the workers in the last century as well as at the turn of the present century.

'*A typical recipe for home-made ginger beer went as follows. A large lemon was peeled thinly and then sliced: both the slices and rind were placed in a large bowl with 1 ounce of best ground ginger, half an ounce of cream of tartar and one pound of sugar. As a rule, one gallon of boiling water was poured over the contents and left to stand until the liquid was luke-warm. Less than half an ounce of German yeast beaten to a cream with a little fine sugar was prepared beforehand and spread on a piece of toast which was allowed to float on the liquid. The bowl was left in a moderately warm place for a day, whereupon a skimming process took place. Finally the mixture was strained and bottled. Stone bottles with screw caps were best and the ginger beer was to be kept in a cool place for a day or so before being used.*' From The Story of Swansea's Districts and Villages, *by Norman Lewis Thomas. Qualprint (Wales) Ltd, Swansea, 1969.*

GINGER BEER

From the manuscript book of Miss M. E. Curtis, 1852, Carno, Montgomeryshire

4 lb. lump sugar	6 oz. stem ginger
6 lemons	4 gallons water
4 oz. yeast	

Peel the lemons, cut them in halves, squease [sic] them on the sugar – bruise the ginger and let them all be in a pan. Then pour the boiling water on them. When cold enough add a small tea-cup full of Yeast. Let it stand 24 hours, then bottle it, in three days it will be fit to drink.

An interesting alternative recipe uses a 10-pint saucepan half-filled with dandelions and nettles in equal proportions, 2 sticks of rhubarb, a handful of blackcurrant leaves, and 4 lumps of well-pounded stem ginger all covered with cold water and boiled for 15 minutes. When this has been strained, 1 lb. lump sugar is added, dissolved, and well stirred. Then 8 pints of cold water are poured over and when tepid, 1 oz. yeast is dissolved in a cup of the liquid and stirred in. It is left overnight, then the yeast skimmed off, and the ginger beer bottled. It should be corked loosely at first, then tightly when bubbling has subsided.

Dowlais Iron Company blast furnace, c. 1870

The Gymnasts, c. *1892*

CIG OEN Â MÊL – HONEYED LAMB

3–4 lb. shoulder of spring lamb
2 level tablespoons rosemary
salt and freshly ground black
  pepper
1 teaspoon ginger

8 oz. (1 cup generous) thick
  honey
½ pint (1 cup) cider approx.
foil

First line the baking tin with foil, as the honey can make it very sticky. Rub the shoulder all over with salt, pepper and the ginger, then put into the baking tin and sprinkle half the finely chopped rosemary over the top. Coat the top skin with honey and pour the cider around. Bake in a hot oven (400° F.) for ½ hour then lower the heat to 325° F. and cook for a further 1¼ hours. Fifteen minutes before it is ready baste carefully and sprinkle over the remaining rosemary. Add a little more cider if it appears to be drying up. Pour off any excess fat from the gravy and reduce slightly on top of the stove, adding more cider if it has evaporated. Serve the sauce separately in a warmed gravy boat.

Chicken or pork can be cooked the same way.

Serves about 6.

The cleanly picked right blade bone of a shoulder of mutton was formerly used for fortune telling in many parts of Wales. This is first mentioned by Gerald the Welshman (*Itinerary Through Wales*, 1188), and Marie Trevelyan in *Folk-lore and Folk Stories of Wales* still found it practised early in this century. It seems, in the main, to have been used on Hallowe'en as a means of divining a future husband. The following rhyme was chanted after the blade bone had been pricked nine times, a magical number in Welsh mythology:

> With this knife this bone I mean to pick:
> With this knife my lover's heart I mean to prick,
> Wishing him neither rest nor sleep
> Until he comes to me to speak.

Onions were also used for similar divination: Up till 1900, girls in farmhouses would name onions after bachelors of the district, then they would be stored in a loft. The first onion to sprout meant that the named one would soon declare his love. If it didn't sprout at all, it signified that he would remain a bachelor.

In the first half of the nineteenth century love-potions consisting of metheglin (*see* page 116), mead, rhubarb, cowslip or primrose wine were put into a drinking horn with a cake made from small pieces of dough kept from nine bakings. This was proffered to an indifferent lover or husband. Up until 1850, a leek was thrown into a loving cup at Courts Leet in Glamorgan. Courtship was taken very seriously!

Welsh kitchen with settle or box beds, Rhiwgraidd, Lledrod

PUNCHNEP

Nep was the old name for some root vegetables, i.e. parsnep or turnnep. This is a simple vegetable dish which has a delicious flavour.

1 lb. potatoes	1 lb. young white turnips
water	salt and pepper
2 tablespoons butter	4 tablespoons warm cream

Boil the potatoes and turnips separately in salted water: this is important to get the right flavour. Drain them well, then mash them separately, adding pepper to taste and dividing the butter between each vegetable. Combine when this is done and beat well together so that the mixture looks like alabaster. Put into a deep, warm bowl, then prod about 6 or 8 small holes down through the purée. Into these holes pour the warm cream, and serve hot. Melted butter can be used in place of cream, but my preference is for plain yoghurt which has been brought to room temperature.

Serves 4–6.

TEISEN NIONOD – ONION CAKE

Very like the French *Pomme de terre à la Boulangère*.

2 lb. peeled and finely sliced potatoes	1 lb. peeled and finely chopped onion
4 oz. (½ cup) butter	salt and pepper

Well grease a fireproof dish and on the bottom lay a thick layer of potato, well seasoned, then a layer of onion. Dot each layer with butter, and repeat this again, or until the dish is full, ending with a layer of potato. The top layer should also be dotted with butter, using more than given above, if necessary. Cover with a lid or foil and bake in a moderate oven (350° F.) for about 1½ hours, removing the lid for the last ½ hour. The variety of potato makes it impossible to give a precise cooking time: very floury ones can cook in 1 hour whereas waxy ones will take longer.

Serves 4–6.

Potato and onion prepared as above, put into a meat roasting-tin with stock to cover, all well seasoned, are very good if a small joint of lamb is roasted on top. The lamb should not be too fat, but if young and lean the juices will run down into the vegetables giving them an excellent flavour. Also the meat will be succulent and free of fat. Serve with a green salad.

Caerphilly cheese originates in Caerphilly, Glamorgan. It is a moist, light cheese which matures in a few weeks. Teisen Nionod can also be made interspersed with grated cheese on each layer, then baked as above.

PASTAI GOCOS – COCKLE PIE

Pen-clawdd means 'Head of the Dyke' and is the last village of north Gower before the peninsula joins the mainland. For many centuries vast cockle-beds have stretched out into the Burry Estuary, and the cockle-women rode out on ponies or donkeys to gather their harvest in wicker baskets. The shellfish lie a few inches below the muddy sand: gatherers use a sharp sickle-shaped piece of iron to cut up the sand, then they scoop the cockles towards them with a scraper and put them into sieves before sluicing with sea-water. Nowadays the cockle industry has been modernized, but Pen-clawdd is still the chief centre. See also page 36.

Traditional

Clams, mussels, limpets or scallops can be used for these recipes, or a mixture of all or several.

TO PREPARE COCKLES

Scrub the shells well to get rid of sand and grit. Then put into a large saucepan, with preferably sea-water (or salted water) barely to cover. Put a lid on, then bring to boiling point, and continue boiling for 2 minutes or until the shells are open. Leave until cool enough to handle, then remove from the shells with a sharp knife. Strain, and reserve cockle liquor.

Once prepared they can be eaten cold with lemon juice or vinegar, or heated in a little butter, pepper and salt and lemon juice, or made into soup (*see* page 15) or Cockle Cakes (page 36).

FOR THE PIE

8 oz. short-crust pastry (*see* page 63)
3 tablespoons chopped chives, spring onions, or green onion tops
8 oz. streaky bacon or salt pork cut into dice
½ pint (1 cup) cockle stock
3 pints (4 cups) approx. cooked prepared cockles
pepper
a little milk

Take a deep pie-dish, damp the sides and line with thickly rolled short-crust pastry, leaving only enough for thin strips on top. Put a layer of cockles on the bottom, then a layer of chopped chives, then bacon, all seasoned with pepper, and repeat this until the dish is full, ending with a layer of cockles. Pour over the cockle stock. Damp the edges of the pastry and lay strips across, lattice fashion. Brush over with milk and bake in a hot oven (400° F.) for about ½ hour or until the pastry is golden. Serve hot or cold, with salad.

Serves 4.

1 or 2 hard-boiled eggs cut into quarters can be added if cockles are in short supply, and canned or bottled cockles can be used, but if bottled in vinegar, wash them first and add 4 tablespoons of milk to the pie.

Pen-clawdd, Glamorgan, cockle-beds and cockle-women, c. 1850

CAWS POBI – WELSH RAREBIT

Wrexham is the burial place of Elihu Yale. His father emigrated from Plas-yn-Ial House to North America in 1637, and Elihu was born in Boston, Massachusetts, soon afterwards. Elihu Yale was the founder of Yale University for in 1691 he sent a cargo of books and Indian goods from Fort Madras, India, where he was governor. These were sold for over five hundred pounds, which initiated the university in 1692. Yale University has a Wrexham Tower in the Memorial Quadrangle. His tomb is inscribed as follows:

> *'Born in America, in Europe bred,*
> *In Africa travelled and in Asia wed,*
> *Where long he lived and thrived; in*
> *   London dead.*
> *Much good, some ill he did; so hope's*
> *   all even,*
> *And that his soul through mercy's gone*
> *   to heaven.*
> *You that survive and read his tale take care*
> *For this most certain exit to prepare.*
> *When blest in peace, the actions of the just*
> *Smell sweet and blossom in the silent dust.'*

'I am a Welshman. I do love cause boby [sic], *good roasted cheese.'* First Boke of the Introduction of Knowledge, *Andrew Boorde, 1547.*

'… " Ten cookes in Wales," quoth he, " one wedding sees." " True," quoth the other, " each man toasts his cheese."' Springes for Woodcockes, *1613, on an Englishman and a Welshman vying as to which of their lands maintained the greatest state.*

Perhaps the most famous of all Welsh dishes and one that has, together with Irish Stew and Haggis, travelled the world over. Family recipe.

8 oz. grated, strong cheese such as Cheddar or Cheshire
1 tablespoon butter
2 teaspoons Worcestershire sauce
1 level teaspoon dry mustard
2 teaspoons flour
4 tablespoons beer (or milk)
shake of pepper
4 slices bread toasted on 1 side only

Put the cheese, flour, mustard, Worcestershire sauce, butter and pepper into a saucepan. Mix well, then add the beer or milk to moisten. Do not make it too wet. Stir over a gentle heat until all is melted, and when it is a thickish paste stop stirring, and swivel it around the saucepan, which it will do quite easily. Leave to cool a little, and meanwhile toast the bread on one side only. Spread the rarebit over the untoasted side and brown under a hot grill. This mixture can be made and kept in the refrigerator for several days if required. Sweet white wine can be used instead of beer and gives a good flavour.

BUCK RAREBIT

Buck Rarebit is Welsh Rarebit, as above, served with a poached egg on top. My Great-aunt Polly Mary used to make her own version, which was 8 oz. cheese with 2 slices of Welsh bacon and a small onion, all minced and mixed well. This was spread on toast and baked in a hot oven until bubbling. It was a great favourite with Uncle George as well as the children.

The Horticulturists, Wrexham, Denbighshire, c. 1910

TEISEN GALAN YSTWYLL – TWELFTH NIGHT CAKE

Twelfth Night, the eve of the Feast of the Epiphany, was formerly celebrated with far more feasting and merrymaking than Christmas which, in Wales, was observed more as a religious ceremony. Twelfth Night was celebrated by a rich cake or, in farmhouses, a pile of cakes, and concealed inside was a dried bean and a pea, the finders being named King Bean and Queen Marrowfat, or the King and Queen of Misrule, who then set the pace for the evening. This is a good rich fruit cake useful for any festive occasion. Recipe from *Country Feasts and Festivals.*

1 lb. (2 cups) butter	6 tablespoons brandy
1 lb. (2 cups) sugar	4 oz. (1 cup) ground almonds
½ teaspoon each of powdered cinnamon, ginger and coriander	4 oz. each minced candied citron and lemon peel
¼ oz. allspice	1 lb. (2 cups) currants
9 separated eggs	1 lb. (2 cups) sultanas (seedless raisins)
1 lb. (4 cups) self-raising flour	pinch of salt

First prepare a 9-in. cake tin by lining it with buttered greaseproof paper. Then cream the butter and sugar, add the spices, then beat in the beaten egg-yolks alternately with the brandy and a dusting of sifted flour. Add the ground almonds, dried fruit and peel. Whip the egg-whites until fairly stiff, then fold into this mixture alternately with the rest of the flour. Add a pinch of salt and mix well. Put into the cake tin and bake in a moderate oven (300° – 350° F.) for 3–4 hours, covering the top with paper for the first 1½ hours. Let it cool slightly in the tin then turn out top downwards onto a wire rack to get cold. It can be brushed with warm apricot jam and covered with marzipan, prior to icing if liked.

ROYAL ICING

4 egg-whites	juice of ½ lemon
1½ lb. sifted icing (confectioner's) sugar	

Beat the egg-whites, adding the sugar by degrees, also the lemon juice, working until the icing is smooth and white. Spread over the cake with a spatula or palette knife and when it is all used, not before, dip the knife in tepid water and smooth all over. When set overnight it will be quite firm.

Miss Vaughan, Dolgellau, Merioneth, 1855

TARTEN GENNIN – LEEK TART OR FLAN

Yet another link with French cooking: this tart is almost identical to the *Flan de Poireaux* of northern France and Brittany.

10 large leeks	FOR THE PASTRY
1 tablespoon butter	6 oz. (1½ cups) flour
4 rashers chopped ham or bacon	3 oz. butter or margarine
2 well-beaten eggs mixed with	a pinch of salt
½ pint (1 cup) cream or milk	about 4 tablespoons iced water
salt and pepper	

First make the pastry by mixing the butter into the flour and salt until it is crumbly. Then add the water and mix well. Keep in a cool place until needed, or if making the flan at once lightly grease an 8-in. flan tin and press the pastry into place after first rolling it roughly. Brush the bottom with a little beaten egg-yolk to prevent it becoming heavy.

Wash and clean the leeks and chop them into 1-in. pieces, leaving on a certain amount of the green part if they are young. Heat the butter and lightly toss the leeks in it, just until they soften – on no account let them brown. Spread this on the pastry, add the diced ham or bacon and season to taste. Beat the eggs with the cream or milk and pour over the leeks and ham, then cook in a moderate oven (350° F.) for about 35 minutes or until the custard is set and slightly golden on top. It can be eaten hot or cold: luke-warm is best I think. Grated cheese can be added if liked, but can spoil the delicate flavour of the leeks. If leeks are not available, then use 2 or 3 medium onions, in which case cheese goes very well with them.

Serves 4.

Cardiff Naturalists' outing to Elan Valley Dam, 1902 (the dams were commenced in 1892 and completed 1907)

Bathing machines, Tenby beach, Pembrokeshire, 1892

SCALLOPS

'*Fish and poultry form a part of every bill of fare. . . .*' Sketches in Wales, *J. W. Harding, 1810.*

All kinds of shellfish are relished in Wales, from the little known razor-shell (Solen siliguia) which can be baked whole in the oven, then sprinkled with pepper, salt, lemon and dotted with butter, to the large king prawn, now very popular all over Wales, and best brushed with oil or butter, sprinkled with herbs and grilled, in their shells for preference, under a hot grill. Tie a napkin round your neck, squeeze some lemon over, have a finger-bowl ready and relish them to the fullest. They are a special feature of The Old Kings Arms Hotel, Pembroke, which is a fourteenth-century coaching inn, kept in excellent repair. Another fourteenth-century pilgrims' rest house, Y Gegin Fawr, at Aberdaron, Caernarvonshire, provides crabs, lobsters and scallops of remarkable size and quality.

The Welsh name for a scallop shell is Cragen Iago, *the shell of St James, and it was used as a badge by pilgrims who went to visit the shrine of St James in Compostella. These shells are used as a small cake tin in Anglesey, at Aberffraw, and the small cakes which resemble shortbread are known as either Aberffraw cakes or* Teisen 'Berffro, *Berffro Cakes.*

SCALLOPS AND BACON

Open the shells with a knife and remove only the small black sac: everything else is edible. If the scallops are very large, cut off the red coral tongue and also cut the white part into two. Barely cover the scallops with water and simmer them for about 10 minutes, then drain but reserve the stock. Take as many skewers as there are people and thread them with: first a bayleaf, then a chunk of coral, a piece of scallop, then a thin piece of bacon, and so on until the skewer is full. Brush with oil and grill on all sides until they are cooked, about 10 minutes, basting at least once with a little of the scallop stock. Keep them warm and add the rest of the stock to the pan juices, and reduce on top of the stove. Serve over the skewers. One large scallop will do per skewer, but if they are scarce, chunks of thick white fish such as halibut, turbot or bass can be interspersed with the scallops and bacon and cooked as above.

TEISEN 'BERFFRO

Use the deep side of the scallop shell as patty tins.

8 oz. (1 cup) butter   8 oz. (1 cup) sugar
8 oz. (2 cups) sifted self-raising
   flour

Cream the butter and sugar together, then work in the flour gradually with the hands, as for a shortbread. Roll out gently and press into the scallop shells, then bake in a moderate oven (325° F.) for about 15–20 minutes. Remove from the shell, and on the curved, fan-like marked side sprinkle coarse sugar. If scallop or large clam shells are not available, it can be rolled out and cut into rounds, but the charm is in the shape and pattern.

Makes about 8.

CIG MOCH WEDI EI FERWI Â SAWS PERSLI – BOILED HAM AND PARSLEY SAUCE

This is perhaps the most traditional method of serving ham in Wales, and very good it is. Especially if *Trolennod Blawd Ceirch*, small fruit-studded, oatmeal dumplings, are added to the stock and served with the meat. These little dumplings are good in any broth-like soup and are easy to make.

TROLENNOD BLAWD CEIRCH

12 oz. (3 cups) fine oatmeal	4 oz. (1 cup) self-raising flour
3 oz. (¾ cup) suet or margarine	2 oz. (½ cup) currants
pinch of salt	approx. 1 cup water or butter-milk

Mix all dry ingredients together, then add just enough liquid to make it firm. Roll in oatmeal-covered hands to small balls about the size of a large walnut, and poach them in stock for about 40 minutes. Drain before serving, and do not let the pot get overcrowded or they may break up.

HAM COOKED WITH CIDER

Ham cooked with cider served with Raisin and Celery sauce was a favourite with Uncle George, and still is with me.

Piece of ham 4–5 lb. soaked overnight in cold water	½ lemon
1 large onion stuck with cloves	1 teaspoon brown sugar
	1 pint cider and water

Put the ham into a large saucepan with all above ingredients, bringing the liquid up with water to barely cover. Bring to the boil, then simmer gently for 25 minutes to the pound. Let it cool in the stock, then peel off the skin; reserve the stock. Mix together:

2 tablespoons brown sugar	3 tablespoons crisp breadcrumbs
½ teaspoon mace	1 teaspoon made mustard

Press this mixture into the ham fat, and moisten with a very little stock. Line a baking tin with foil and put the ham in with about ½ pint (1 cup) of stock around, and bake in a moderate (375° F.) oven for about 30 minutes.
Meanwhile make the sauce:

SAUCE INGREDIENTS

2 stalks celery, chopped	1 tablespoon flour
2 oz. seedless raisins	1 tablespoon butter
½ pint (1 cup) ham stock	pepper

Melt the butter and stir in the flour, then add the warm ham stock and stir briskly to avoid lumps. Add all other ingredients and simmer for about 10 minutes. Do not overcook for it is the crispness of the celery that acts as a foil to the sweet ham.

Serves 6.

PARSLEY SAUCE

Parsley sauce is also served with boiled chicken and poached salmon. Use whatever stock the food has been cooked in, otherwise the method is the same as above, but use ½ cup freshly chopped parsley instead of the celery and raisins. For salmon and chicken, flavour with a pinch of mace or nutmeg, and garnish with 2 tablespoons of fresh cream.

Before the supermarket, Commercial Street, Maesteg, Glamorgan, c. 1900

L AWR – LAVER

'A capital dinner! you don't get moor mutton, with hot laver sauce every day!' Collins, *1875*.

Laver (*Porphyra laciniata*) and green laver (*Ulva latissima*) are the same as Sloke in Ireland and Scotland, but they are in much greater daily use in South Wales, particularly in the Swansea and south Pembrokeshire districts. Laver is a smooth fine seaweed, sometimes called sea-spinach, which clings to the rocks like silk. It was cured in drying houses as in the photograph, but nowadays more scientific methods are used. It is sold in Swansea market and many other places already prepared, when it resembles a dark, brownish, spinach-like gelatine purée, ready for use. It can be supplied by James Howell Ltd, Cardiff.

Bara Lawr – Laverbread – is a misleading name for it does not resemble bread at all but the purée described above. Contrary to what one would expect, it doesn't taste fishy; perhaps a vague caviar-like taste can be discerned. If found in its natural state it must be well washed to remove all sand and grit. Then it is boiled in water to cover for at least 5–6 hours, before draining. After that has been done, it has many uses. All mixing is traditionally done with wooden or silver spoons and aluminium saucepans.

To make Laver Sauce, mix the prepared laver with a squeeze of bitter orange juice, butter, and some gravy from the lamb or mutton, all well seasoned. This sauce is also good with lobster or other shellfish, substituting cream for the mutton gravy. The sauce can also be served on toast or in sandwiches, and mixed with lemon juice and a little olive oil it makes an *hors-d'œuvre*.

Mix prepared laverbread with a good sprinkling of fine oatmeal, then shape into little cakes and fry in bacon fat; or coat the laver-bread in oatmeal, fry in fat and serve with grilled ham or bacon, sprinkled with a little onion juice or lemon.

It also makes a good soup, if about $\frac{1}{2}$ cup is added to Welsh Cawl (*see* page 35) then either sieved or liquidized: laver can be added to any fish or chowder with advantage, in the above quantity. Do not overdo the flavour, for it is an acquired taste like caviar, olives, or oysters, but once acquired it can become a passion. It has, needless to say, great health-giving properties and was regularly eaten in the fashionable eighteenth-century spa at Bath.

Laverbread curing, Freshwater West, Pembrokeshire, c. 1900

Bara

Bara – bread – is of excellent quality all over Wales: baking is an art which has not been forgotten in the Principality. There are at least twenty (and probably more) different shapes and kinds of loaves found generally in shops, even today; *bara Abertawe* (Swansea bread), *bara tun* (tin bread) and *bara fflat* (batch loaf) are but a few. *Bara planc* is bread cooked on a bakestone or *planc* (*see* page 2). Formerly baking was done for the household about once a week, and old kitchens always had a carved wooden crate suspended from the ceiling, known as a bread crate or car, in which the bread was put and kept safe from mice, beetles or even domestic animals. Similarly there was a rack suspended from the ceiling to hang sides, hams or pieces of ham or bacon from. In some cases these crates could be lowered by pulleys, but in humbler dwellings it was necessary to stand on the table to remove or put in the loaves. Bread was generally baked in stone ovens (which gave the crisp crust) heated with faggots of wood, and when the hot ashes were removed the bread was placed inside, after which the opening was closed with a metal plate and often sealed with clay. Dough was often broken into large pieces, some being put aside to have currants and spices pitched into it, thus making a fruited bun-loaf. *See Bara Brith, page 108.*

BARA GWENITH

Bara Gwenith – Wholemeal bread.
Recipe from Miss Rosemary Leach.

3 lb. (12 cups) wholemeal flour	1 heaped tablespoon lard or other fat
1 tablespoon black treacle (molasses)	1 oz. dried yeast
a pinch of salt	approx. 1¼ pints of warm water in all
1 heaped teaspoon brown sugar	

See that all utensils and ingredients are warm.

Rub the fat into the warmed flour, then dissolve the yeast and sugar in approximately ¼ pint (½ cup) luke-warm water and allow it to froth up. Add the yeast mixture to flour and mix the dough with more warm water in which the treacle and salt have already been dissolved. It will probably require about 1¼ pints in all. Add a very little more water if the dough seems too stiff but on no account make it sloppy. Knead for 5 minutes, then divide the dough into two and place into two greased, warmed loaf tins (about 10 in. by 4 in.). Cut three slanting nicks across the tops of the loaves and put in a warm place, with a cloth on top, for about an hour, or until the dough has almost doubled in size. Pre-heat the oven to 425° F. and put the loaves in, then 10 minutes later reduce the heat to 400° F. for another 30–35 minutes. Turn out of the tins and cool on a wire rack. The loaves sound hollow when tapped on the bottom if properly cooked.

Makes 2 loaves.

The Miller and his wife, Edern, c. 1900

The handwritten ledger (left)

From the Home Farm
334 Chickens @ 3/   50 2 :
    9 Turkeys @ ?/   2 16 :
    5 Guinea Fowls @ 3/   : 15 :
1603 lbs: of Beef (2 Cows) @ 17½   49 5 3
 107 lbs: of Veal (2 Calves) @ 1/10   9 3 3
1368 lbs: of Mutton @ 9½ } 20 Sheep 54 1 "
  55 lbs: of Lamb @ 1/- }
 109 lbs: of Fresh Butter @ 1/4   7 5 4
2050 Fresh Eggs @ 16 & 17/   6 9 2
 450 Quarts new milk @ 4d a qt   7 10 "
 146 Quarts of old Milk @ 2d "   1 4 4
 171 Pints of Cream @ 8 a pint   5 5 6
  90 Stone (1260 lbs:) of Potatoes   2 14 "
  84 Bushels of Oats @ 3/6   14 14 "
  35 lot: of Hay @ 4/- a lot: 7 " "
                                  £218. 4. 4

Butchers Bills   60 " "
Beer. 11 Hogsheads   37 16 "
Champagne. 60 Doz: 180 " "
Other Liquors. Wines Spirits. 30 Doz: 30 " "
Groceries Mr. Hall £70 Mr. Higgins £34 } 120 7 "   £646 7
    Mrs. Davis £11.7.0 }

Withers from London. (Cooks Waiters &c) 416 "
    (Ices & Confectionery)
Tansley. Ball room   158 "
Wilder. Fireworks & Illuminations 180 0
Band   56 "
Teague. Tents - Waiters &c   37 "
J.W. Ry: Carriage of Ball room &c 34 5
Phillips & Howse for Canvas. Matters &c 25 12
Waugh. May Dances   24 "
Hire of Chairs   15 15
Capt: Berthon - Constables   7 "
Lewis. Decorations. Arches &c   6 10
                             £1606. 9

Pair of Pictures (Mrs. R.)   140. 0
                                90. 0
Piano (Mrs. R.)   10. 0
Self recording Barometer (from his Brothers & Sisters)
                             £1846. 9

Spiced Beef (right)

SPICED BEEF

6 lb. boned rib of beef, or rump
½ lb. coarse salt
4 oz. (½ cup) soft brown sugar
½ oz. (1 level tablespoon) saltpetre
2 teaspoons each of ground black pepper, cloves, allspice and mace

3 tablespoons beef dripping or oil
1 large onion, sliced
6 sliced carrots
1 bayleaf
1 pint (2 cups) stock

Mix the salt, sugar, saltpetre and spices together, put the meat in a deep earthenware dish and rub the salt mixture all over it. Cover and leave for 10 days, turning the meat each day and rubbing the salt mixture well over all the joint. At the end of that time, remove the meat and wash thoroughly, dab it dry with kitchen paper, and tie up into a convenient carving shape. Heat the beef dripping in a heavy fireproof pot and lightly fry the bayleaf, onion and carrots, and when the onion is soft put the joint on the bed of vegetables, and pour the stock around. Transfer the pot or casserole to a moderate oven (300°–325° F.) and cook for about 4 hours. Lower the heat after 1 hour to about 250° F. and check from time to time that the liquid has not dried up; if it has add a little more. This spiced beef should be so tender that it can be pulled with a fork. Either serve hot, as it is, or turn out into a deep dish, pour the strained juice over, put a plate on top and then a weight. Leave overnight, and serve cold, cut into slices.

Serves about 8.

Left: *Expenses at The Hendre on the occasion of the Coming of Age of John Maclean Rolls*   *April 1891*

Right: *Roasting the ox on the occasion of John Maclean Rolls, of The Hendre, Monmouth, coming-of-age, April 25th 1891*

PWDIN CAWS POBI CYMREIG – WELSH CHEESE PUDDING

Adapted from *Y Ty a'r Teulu* by Mrs S. M. Mathews, 1891.

4 thick slices crustless bread
butter
8 oz. grated Cheddar or other
hard, strong cheese
1 egg

1 pint (2 cups) milk, or half milk
and half cream
a pinch of nutmeg
½ teaspoon dry mustard
pepper and cayenne pepper

Lightly toast the bread on *one side only*, and butter them on the untoasted side. Grease a round ovenproof dish and lay two of them, toast side down, on the bottom, and on top put half the grated cheese sprinkled with half the seasonings. Add the 2 remaining slices of buttered toast, buttered side upwards, then scatter over the rest of the cheese. Bring the milk just to the boil, add the remaining seasonings, beat the egg and pour the hot milk over it. Pour this over the cheese pudding and let it stand for at least ½ hour, or longer if necessary, to let the bread soak up the liquid. Bake for ½ hour in a moderate oven (350° F.) until it is puffed up and golden on top. Serve hot.

Makes about 2 portions if for a light meal, but as a savoury it will serve 4.

At Tenby Races, Pembrokeshire, 1912

Salmon Netting, Teifi Estuary, Cardiganshire, 1881

EOG RHOST – ROAST SALMON

As well as being fished from coracles (see page 30) large numbers of salmon are netted in the Teifi estuary and elsewhere in Wales.
'For dinner we had salmon and leg of mutton . . .'
George Borrow, Wild Wales, *1862.*

Eog rhost – roast salmon, an old Welsh way of cooking salmon employing the herbs and spices so loved by the Welsh people.

1 salmon grilse about 4–5 lb., or a tail-end about 3 lb.	4 oz. (½ cup), plus 1 tablespoon butter
½ teaspoon nutmeg (grated)	1 tablespoon vinegar
2 cloves	½ large sliced orange
2 bayleaves spread with butter	½ finely sliced lemon
1-in. sprig of fresh rosemary	salt and pepper

Season the salmon well inside and out with salt and pepper and rub in the nutmeg. Tuck the buttered bayleaves, rosemary and cloves into the gullet, or if using a cut of salmon put the bayleaves underneath and then the other spices and herbs on top. Rub the 4 oz. butter over all, cover with paper or foil and roast in a moderate oven (350° F.) for 20 minutes to the pound, basting it at least once with the juices. When ready, remove the fish to a warmed dish, and peel off the skin. Put the pan on top of the stove add the tablespoon of butter in small pieces, the very thin slices of orange and lemon, and the vinegar, let it boil up quickly and reduce on a fast flame until the orange is soft and slightly brown at the edges and the gravy is reduced by about half. Serve separately in a sauceboat, first removing the lemon and orange slices and placing them alternately along the back of the fish.

Serves 8–10.

Left-over Salmon is very good cut into pieces, dipped in batter (*see* page 36) and served with Granville Sauce (*see* page 44).

HWYADEN HALLT CYMREIG – WELSH SALT DUCK WITH ONION SAUCE

Singleton Park, the birthplace and home of Henry Hussey Vivian (afterwards 1st Baron Swansea) is now part of Swansea University College centre.

Traditional

This most original and delicious way of serving duck is still to be found in Wales, yet nowhere else in the British Isles. Large fat ducks are essential to this dish: ducklings are better treated in the more usual ways.

1 large duck or 2 smaller ducks
½ lb. (½ cup) sea-salt per duck
giblets boiled in 1½ pints
   (3 cups) water

1 pint (2 cups) giblet stock
1 sliced onion
pepper

Put the duck or ducks, the giblets removed, in a deep dish then rub the sea-salt all over. Cover with a cloth and leave in a cool place for 2–3 days, turning over and rubbing the salt in twice a day during this time. Then rinse the duck, pat it dry and put into a large casserole, arrange the sliced onion around, season with pepper and pour the stock over. Put the lid on and cook in a moderate oven (350° F.) for about 2 hours. Half cider and half stock can be used if preferred.

SAWS NIONOD – ONION SAUCE

If serving hot, onion sauce is the traditional accompaniment and is made as follows:

1 lb. finely sliced onions
½ pint (1 cup) stock from the duck

½ pint (1 cup) light cream, cream or top of the milk
1 heaped tablespoon butter
1 heaped tablespoon flour

Simmer the finely sliced onions in the stock from the duck, seasoning to taste, for about ½ hour or until they are quite soft. In another saucepan heat the butter, stir in the flour, let it cook for 1 minute then add the strained liquor from the onions, stirring all the time until you have a smooth sauce. Add the onions, mix well and then add the cream or creamy milk, stirring until it is all amalgamated.

Salt duck is excellent served cold: in this case leave it to get cold in the stock, then skin and arrange it on a dish, and serve with an oil and vinegar dressing as follows:

1 teaspoon dry mustard powder
6 tablespoons olive oil
salt and pepper

1 teaspoon made French mustard
3 tablespoons wine vinegar

Mix the 2 mustards together and add a little salt. Then mix in the oil and vinegar. Shake well, and season with pepper to taste.

Lord Gordon-Lennox and Glynn Vivian (brother of the photographer, Henry H. Vivian), Singleton Park, Swansea, c. 1850

CIG OEN RHOST Â SAWS CRIAFOL –
ROAST SADDLE OF MUTTON WITH ROWANBERRY SAUCE

'. . . As for the leg of mutton it is truly wonderful; nothing so good had I ever tasted in the shape of a leg of mutton. The leg of mutton of Wales beats the leg of mutton of any other country, and I had never tasted a Welsh leg of mutton before. Certainly I shall never forget the first Welsh leg of mutton which I tasted, rich but delicate, replete with juices derived from the aromatic herbs of the noble Berwyn, cooked to a turn, and weighing just four pounds.' George Borrow, Wild Wales, 1862.

The small Welsh sheep graze on the wild mountain thyme which gives the meat a characteristic flavour. The joints are so small that a hindquarter is sometimes cut as a leg. When bred with the larger Shropshire and Kerry the animals are bigger, but the taste is not improved. Saddle of lamb or mutton (both sides of the loin joined together), normally too large a joint for the average family, becomes a reasonable joint when taken from a Welsh sheep.

---

1 saddle weighing about 8–9 lb. (half a saddle or loin about 4–5 lb. can be used for a smaller family). The kidneys are usually dressed on top of the joint at the tail end. As they become over-cooked if roasted with the joint, it is wise to remove them, but add them to the pan about $\frac{1}{2}$ hour before the joint is ready, then affix them with small skewers before serving.

rosemary	a pinch	flour
thyme	of each,	mace or nutmeg
parsley	finely	4 tablespoons mutton dripping or oil
mint	chopped	salt
marjoram	or	pepper
garlic	powdered	$\frac{1}{4}$ pint ($\frac{1}{2}$ cup) cider, or ale or red wine

Mountain meat is very lean, so needs more basting than the fatter valley animals. First rub the entire joint with pepper, mace or nutmeg and the powdered herbs, then spread over the dripping or oil, and dredge the top skin liberally with flour. Set in a moderate oven (350° F.) and roast for 20 minutes to the pound if you like your meat pink, and 25 minutes if liked well done. Twenty minutes before it is ready, baste well, dust again with flour and sprinkle the crust with a few drops of ice-cold water to crisp it. Pour off the excess fat from the pan and add (traditionally) a glass of cider or ale, but a glass of red wine gives an excellent flavour. Dilute this with about $\frac{1}{2}$ pint (1 cup) water and set it back in the oven. When ready, put the joint on a warmed dish and secure the kidneys at the tail end, then reduce the gravy on top of the stove for about 10 minutes. A saddle is carved in slices parallel to the backbone, although it can be carved down into large cutlets.

Serve with Saws Criafol – see page 32. Serves 8–10.

Stage coach outside the King's Head, Newport, Monmouthshire, c. 1890

TAFELL O GIG LLO RHOST – ROAST FILLET OF VEAL

From *The First Principles of Good Cookery*, by Lady Llanover, 1867.

1 3-lb. fillet or boned loin of veal
½ lb. fat pork or bacon cut into slices
1 pint (2 cups) water
¼ pint (½ cup) sherry

FOR THE STUFFING
3 oz. (1 cup) breadcrumbs, moistened with 2 tablespoons milk
2 tablespoons grated suet or melted butter
white part of 1 leek, chopped
½ teaspoon chopped thyme
pinch of nutmeg
salt and pepper

Mix all the stuffing ingredients together and stuff the boned joint. Put the joint into a baking tin and put the fat pork or bacon crisscross over the top. Pour the water around, cover with foil and bake in a moderate oven (350° F.) for 1½ hours. Remove the foil for the last ½ hour to allow the top to brown. Add the sherry to the pan juices and reduce rapidly on top of the stove. Serve with the following Welsh veal sauce.

SURYN CYFFAITH POETH – WELSH VEAL SAUCE

This is a sauce which can be made well ahead of time and kept in screwtop bottles; it will keep for years.

3 lemons
1 oz. grated horseradish
½ lb. coarse salt
2 pints (4 cups) vinegar
1 heaped teaspoon each of ground mace, cayenne pepper and whole cloves
1 tablespoon dry mustard

Cut the unpeeled lemons into small pieces and cover with the salt, then add all other ingredients and put into a large ovenproof dish with a lid. Stand in another dish with water coming up to within 2 inches of the first container, bring to the boil and boil steadily for 15–20 minutes. Remove the container with the sauce, leave the lid on and put into a cool place. Stir well once every day for 6 weeks, but replace the lid. Bottle at the end of this time, and screw down tightly. It is excellent with either hot or cold veal and a little goes a long way. It is not unlike the *Vinaigrette* sauce served in Brittany with roast veal and *tête de veau* (à la vinaigrette).

TO STEW A BREAST OF VEAL

Recipe from the manuscript of Anne Wynne of Bodewryd, 1675, later Madam Owen of Penrhos, Anglesea [sic].

'Take a brest of veal and score it and flower it, put a good quantity of butter in yr pan, where yr liquid is hott, put the brest in it and let it fry till it be very brown – turning it often – then take brest and clean it from the liquor and clean the pan, then put a good quantity of claret with some cloves, mace, nutmegs into yr pan, with pickled oysters, 2 anchovies, and a shallot. Let yr brest stew in it, and when it is stewed enough, serve it up with sliced lemon – claret or cider will do.'

FISH

Fishing is as popular in Wales as it is in France: fishing not only as a pastime, for the catch is not displayed, perhaps later to be stuffed and hung in a glass case, but invariably cooked and eaten fresh. Even in the sad days of the depression in the twenties and thirties many miners or quarrymen would go down to a stream or lake to fish for the Sunday morning breakfast. Those lakes and streams contain fishes known only to Wales in many cases: the *torgoch*, a red-bellied char, and *gwyniad* found in Lake Bala, both trapped there by the Ice Age; brown trout (so superior to the North American rainbow trout imported into many waterways in the twenties because of their ability to live in muddy waters), said to have been introduced into many lakes in the thirteenth century by the Cistercian monks of Strata Florida (Cardiganshire). Many of these lakes such as the Teifi pools, Gwyn Lake, Gwenog and Llyn Berwyn are still well stocked. In the seventeenth century the Vicar of Llanwenog wrote about the fish having gold or silver collars: this was however a medieval practice with pike and carp, similar to the way we tag fish today.

Giraldus Cambrensis (Gerald the Welshman) writing about 1188 says: 'The salmon of the Wye are in season during the winter, those of the Usk in summer; but the Wye alone produces the fish called Umber [grayling] the praise of which is celebrated in the works of Ambrosius.... "What", says he, "is more beautiful to behold, more agreeable to smell, or more pleasant to taste? The famous lake of Brecheinoc supplies the country with pike, perch, excellent trout, tench and eels."'

The grayling has a fragrant smell of wild thyme and cucumber.

The delicate and beautiful salmon- or sea-trout is known as *sewin* in Wales and is often caught from coracles (*see* page 30). The Dovey River, George Borrow's 'Royal Dyfi', is thought to be the finest river in Britain for catching it, as well as brown or river trout.

'What a breakfast! Pot of hare; ditto of trout;[1]
pot or prepared shrimps; dish of plain shrimps;
tin of sardines, beautiful beefsteak; eggs, muffin;
large loaf and butter, not forgetting capital tea.
There's a breakfast for you!'

George Borrow, *Wild Wales*, 1862

[1] Potted trout can be made the same way as Potted Herrings, page 53. *See also* Shrimp Paste, page 41.

Boiling up the Brewis Kettle, Singleton Park, near Swansea, c. 1842; photographer, Henry H. Vivian

Brewis

Brewis *or* brywes *was a tea-kettle broth, not unlike* sowans *in Ireland and Scotland: the nearest equivalent today is milk toast. Originally it was made from oat husks, but later from* bara ceirch, *oat bread, crumbled up in a pot with boiling water poured over it. The pot was covered and the brewis cooked over a wood or peat fire for about a quarter of an hour, then butter and seasonings were added and it was eaten with a wooden or horn spoon so that the mouth would not be burned. Sometimes a lump of bacon would be added if you were lucky. It is not as uninteresting as it sounds and was a great filler-up in the hungry years.*

TEISEN BLAT

Teisen blat is a Plate Cake or tart, also called a Harvest Cake, for large rounds were made for the workers at harvest-time. It is much thinner than an ordinary fruit tart, the pastry being almost wafer-thin, and the fruit inside pre-cooked to a purée. Apples, rhubarb, gooseberries, plums or blaeberries can all be used (or a mixture) according to season. Often the pastry is spiced as follows:

1 lb. (4 cups) self-raising flour	2 teaspoons sugar
8 oz. (1 cup) butter, margarine or lard (or a mixture of all)	$\frac{1}{2}$ teaspoon cinnamon pinch of mixed spice
approx. 8 tablespoons cold water	a little milk

$1\frac{1}{2}$ lb. cooked and sweetened fruit (stoned if using a stone fruit such as plums or apricots) cooked to a purée

Mix the flour with the sugar and spices, rub in the fat. Add the cold water, mixing well until it is a pliable dough. Turn out onto a floured table and roll out very thinly, then cut into 4 rounds. Grease 2 ovenproof flattish plates about 9–10 in. across; damp the edges and lay one piece on each plate, prick the bottom, then put into a hot oven (400° F.) for 10 minutes. Take out and fill with half the fruit to each plate, damp the edges and lay on the tops, pressing down well so that they are secure. Prick the tops lightly, brush with milk and bake in a moderate oven (350° F.) for about 20 minutes or until it is golden brown on top. This tart is often served cold or lukewarm cut into pieces. Buttermilk was frequently drunk with the harvest cake.

BARA BRITH

Bara brith means 'speckled bread' and is common to all the Celtic countries. In Ireland it is called Barm Brack; Selkirk Bannock in Scotland; and Morlaix Brioche in Brittany. It is traditionally made with yeast, but very good bara brith is made using baking powder.

(1)

1 lb. (4 cups) flour	2 heaped tablespoons chopped mixed peel
1 oz. yeast	½ teaspoon mixed ground spice
½ pint (1 cup) luke-warm milk	6 oz. (⅔ cup) seedless raisins
1 teaspoon white sugar	3 tablespoons currants
3 oz. (scant ½ cup) lard or butter	4 tablespoons brown sugar
1 egg	pinch of salt
warm honey to glaze	

See that all utensils and ingredients are warm.

Warm the milk to tepid with the teaspoon of white sugar, crumble in the yeast and set aside for 10–20 minutes until it is frothy. Rub the fat into the flour, then stir in the peel, dried fruit, spices, brown sugar and salt. Make a well in the centre add the yeasted milk and the well-beaten egg. Mix to a soft dough, cover and leave in a warm place to rise for about 2 hours, until it is double its size. Turn onto a floured board and knead well, then put into a well-greased tin, cover again and leave for 30 minutes. Remove cover and put into a hot oven (400° F.) for 20 minutes, then lower the heat to 325° F. and bake for about 1¼ hours. The loaf will sound hollow when tapped on the bottom if it is properly cooked. Put onto a wire rack and brush the top with clear honey whilst it is still warm to give it a nice glaze. Let it get quite cold before cutting, and serve in slices with butter.

(2) Bara brith made without yeast.

From a recipe of Mrs Moir, of Lake Vyrnwy Hotel.

1 lb. (4 cups) self-raising flour	6 tablespoons sugar
1 lb. mixed dried fruit	½ pint (1 cup) warm tea without milk
2 tablespoons marmalade	1 teaspoon mixed ground spice
1 egg	honey to glaze

Mix the dried fruit and sugar together and pour the warm, milkless tea over then leave to stand overnight or for some hours until the fruit is swollen up. The next day stir in the flour, spice, marmalade and finally the well-beaten egg. Line a loaf tin with greased paper, put the mixture in and cook in a moderate oven (325° F.) for 1¾ hours. Turn out onto a wire rack when cooked and brush with warm honey to glaze.

Outing to Aberystwyth, c. 1892

PWDIN MYNWY – MONMOUTH PUDDING

12 oz. (4 cups) fresh white breadcrumbs

3 tablespoons sugar (vanilla sugar
if possible)

4 drops vanilla essence if not
using vanilla sugar

¼ pint (½ cup) boiling milk

2 tablespoons butter, melted

3 stiffly beaten egg-whites

1 lb. raspberry or strawberry
jam

Put the breadcrumbs into a warm basin and pour the boiling milk over using just as much as will lightly soak them but not make them sloppy; cover and leave to stand for 15 minutes, then flake up with a fork. Stir in the sugar and the melted butter, mixing it very lightly. Grease a round ovenproof dish. Whip up the egg-whites, then fold them into the breadcrumb mixture. Put a thick layer of jam on the bottom of the dish, then half the breadcrumb mixture, then another layer of jam and finally the rest of the crumbs. Bake in a slow oven (225°–250° F.) for about 20–30 minutes or until the crumb mixture is just set. Serve either hot or lukewarm. This is a simple way of making a soufflé-like pudding and it is very light and good.

Serves 4.

For festive occasions the jam can be flavoured with a little rum or sherry and mixed with chopped crystallized fruits.

C YW IÂR – SPATCHCOCK

A sixteenth-century recipe seldom served today.

The name derives from 'dispatch-cock', meaning a fowl killed and cooked in a hurry, usually split and grilled. It is a very good way of serving a small broiler chicken, for it cooks quickly, retaining all the flavour and juices. Allow 1 bird of about 2 lb. for 2 people.

2 plump young chickens	1 oz. ($\frac{1}{2}$ cup) fresh breadcrumbs
6 oz. ($\frac{3}{4}$ cup) melted butter	mixed with $\frac{1}{4}$ teaspoon grated
2 teaspoons dry mustard	nutmeg
salt and pepper	2 tablespoons milk

Have the chicken split in two right through the breast bone. Beat each half well with the flat side of a heavy knife. This prevents it curling up when cooking. Place in a grilling tin without the rack and season well. Pour over half the melted butter and cook under the grill for 7–10 minutes starting with inside part of the bird. Do not have the grill too high for fear of burning. Turn and repeat this on the flesh side, pouring over the rest of the butter. Mix the mustard with the milk, making it rather thinner than table mustard. Brush the flesh side of the chicken with this, then sprinkle with the fresh, spiced breadcrumbs. Baste with the butter from the pan, put back under a slow grill and let the top colour slowly to golden.

Serves 4.

CREMPOG – PANCAKES

Pancakes are common to all the Celtic countries : even within those countries, they vary in thickness from the chunky drop-scones of Scotland to the crêpes dentelles of Brittany, which are like fine lace. They have various names in Wales : Pice'r Pregethwr, or pikelets ; Crampoethau, crumpets ; Pancws Llaeth Sur, sour milk pancakes ; or crempog. They differ very little in method or ingredients, only in thickness. Traditionally they were cooked on a bakestone, buttered whilst hot, piled one on top of the other, then cut through into quarters. A heavy frying pan, very slightly greased, can be used if a griddle or bakestone is not available. See also Crempog Geirch, page 53.

CREMPOG Â BWYD MÔR – Pancake with Sea-food
Crempog is very good layered with cooked fish or shellfish: also chopped chicken or ham according to taste.

FOR THE PANCAKES
8 oz. (2 cups) flour
2 eggs
3 tablespoons melted butter or margarine
1 pint (2 cups) buttermilk or milk
pinch of salt

FOR THE FILLING
2 cups cooked, boned and flaked fish, or chopped shellfish – approx. 2 lb. before boning etc.
2 heaped tablespoons grated cheese
½ pint milk
1 heaped tablespoon butter
1 heaped tablespoon flour
a pinch of dry mustard
salt and pepper

To make the pancakes, first beat the eggs well. Pour the melted butter into the salt and flour, then add the eggs, beating well. Gradually pour in the buttermilk, beating all the time so that the mixture is smooth. Leave to stand whilst making the filling, but beat up well before using.

Make the sauce for the filling by heating the butter and stirring in the flour and letting it cook for 1 minute. Pour in the milk, stirring all the time to avoid lumps, then add the seasonings and dry mustard. Finally mix in the fish and the grated cheese and simmer gently until the cheese is melted.

Lightly grease a heavy pan, and pour a tablespoon of the batter in when the pan is hot, tilting it so that the batter runs evenly. Let one side become golden then turn and do the other side. Drain on paper. When all the batter is used, take a deep dish and put in the pancakes layered with the fish and sauce, ending with a pancake on top, masked with a little of the sauce. Put into a slow oven (250° F.) for 15 minutes to heat up. Serve cut into quarters.

Makes about 20 pancakes 4 in. across.

The same batter if slightly sweetened with 3 tablespoons sugar, a pinch of spice, and sometimes a spoonful of currants, can be cooked as above, and served for tea.

Evening at Abersoch, Caernarvonshire, 1900

MEDD HEN FFASIWN – MEAD, OR METHEGLIN IN WALES

In the early years and until the late nineteenth century, Christmas in parts of Wales began at between 3 and 6 a.m. on Christmas morning with a religious service known as plygain. This was preceded by supper parties in large houses, and in humbler homes by decorating the houses or making treacle toffee (cyflaith). Mrs Elizabeth Baker in her diary written between 1778 and 1786 says: '. . . I set forth to celebrate what is here named a Plugen. Coffee and tea commenced it with an abundance of Wiggs, buttered Pikelets and cakes. . . . The cards continued till supper which was a hot and plentiful one and resumed again after: about three in the morning coffee and Tea, etc. was again served . . . and after that was mulled Ebillon and warm Punch for the males. The cards ceased . . . the bell summoned us to church; . . . prayers were begun and the Church quite filled where we stayed till eight and broad daylight, hearing the different carols sung.'

After the plygain *feasting began, consisting of hot ale, toasted cheese and bread in farmhouses; cakes and cold meats,* brewis *in others.*

In Glamorgan and Monmouthshire, Christmas night was enlivened by the Mari Lwyd, but in many other parts of Wales this ceremony was associated with the New Year and Twelfth Night. In any case it carried over several days and the origins are obscure, although it is most likely connected with Celtic pre-Christian horse worship. The name means 'grey Mary', or grey mare, and the protagonists carried round a horse's skull on a pole with a white sheet draped over it, the skull decorated with ribbons, and coloured glass to represent the eyes. The man carrying the Mari Lwyd stood underneath the sheet, holding the pole and moving the lower jaw by means of a wooden handle. The carriers were impromptu poets and singers who challenged those inside to a rhyming contest. The inmates could keep them out so long as they could answer the rhyme, but when this failed the poets would bring in the horse's head, lay it on the table and be entitled to food and drink on the house. By the nineteenth century, traditional rhymes were sung and had to be answered, but many were extempore.

MEAD

1 gallon water
2 pints clear honey
2 lemons
4 cloves

1 lb. white sugar
sprig of rosemary
a piece of root ginger 4 in. long
1 oz. yeast spread on a piece of toast

Boil together the sugar, water and honey and skim off any scum that may form. Stand in an earthenware basin and add the juice of the lemons and the rind of one, also the cloves, rosemary and well-bruised ginger. When this has cooled to blood temperature or less, add the yeast on a piece of toast (if put into too-hot liquid the yeast will be killed). Remove the lemon peel after 3 days, but let fermentation continue until it has stopped 'hissing', after which it should be left for about a week. Strain and bottle, cork loosely to begin with, then tighten up if it is not bubbling. Leave for at least 3–6 months before drinking.

The Mari Lwyd, *Llangynwyd, Glamorgan, 1905; photographer, Llewelyn Evans*

CYFLAITH – TREACLE TOFFEE

In Glamorgan, Carmarthen and Monmouthshire the custom of small boys collecting the Calennig (*New Year's gift*) is still practised although seldom accompanied by the decorated, skewered oranges and apples of the previous and earlier centuries. The fruit was pierced with corn, sometimes coloured, and stuck with three skewers to serve as a stand when not being held, and a fourth which acted as a handle. The top was decorated with holly or mistletoe. Lt-Colonel Llewelyn Evans, who took the accompanying photograph as a very young man, says that it is a survival of the Roman custom of strena, *a pagan symbol of fruitfulness for the coming year. He remembers the Vicar of Llangynwyd*

saying: ' *Ah! the little Llan boys with the Roman* strena *once again.'* The custom of collecting pennies and small cakes started early in the morning and was always finished by noon. Sometimes verses were recited in return for the gift, one being translated as:

' *I got up early and walked as fast as I could to ask for calennig; if you feel it in your heart give me a shilling or sixpence: A Happy New Year for a halfpenny or a penny.*' Bye-gones, *1900.*

---

1 lb. (2 cups) demerara sugar   12 oz. (3 cups) golden syrup
12 oz. (1½ cups) butter   (corn syrup)

Boil all together and stir gently for about 10 minutes, or until a few drops poured into cold water harden at once. Pour into an oiled flat tin or plate, and when barely set mark into squares with a knife and loosen from the bottom of the tin. Leave until quite cold and firm before taking off and breaking up into pieces. Either wrap in small squares of oiled paper or store in an airtight tin. Makes about 2 lb. toffee. Nuts or dried fruit may be added before pouring into the tin, if liked.

Blwyddyn Newydd Dda

Happy New Year

Boys collecting the Calennig, *Llangynwyd, Glamorgan, 1904; photographer, Llewelyn Evans*

'There were jumping sausages, roasting pies,
And longloaves in the bin,
And a stump of Caerphilly to rest our eyes,
And a barrel rolling in.

. . .

'O a ham-bone high on a ceiling-hook
And a goose with a golden skin,
And the roaring flames of the food you cook:
For God's sake let us in!'

Vernon Watkins, from *Ballad of the Mari Lwyd*. Reprinted by
permission of Faber & Faber Ltd.

INDEX

Anchovies. *See* Sgadan Abergwaun, 1
Anglesey Eggs, 23
Apple Sauce, Spicy, 42
Apricocke Wine, 23

Bara, 90
Bara Brith, 108
Bara Ceirch, 2
Bara Gwenith, 90
Bara Lawr, 88
Bara Sinsir, 8
Beef, Spiced, 92
    Welsh Braised, 73
Berdys, 41
Blackberry Curd, 48
    Wine, 48
Boiled Ham and Parsley Sauce, 86
Braised Beef, Welsh, 73
    Game Birds, 6
Bread. *See* Bara
Breast of Veal, Stewed, 103
Brewis, 107
Brithyll â Chig Moch, 16
Buck Rarebit, 78

Cacen Gneifio, 47
Cacs Ffair Llanddarog, 59
Cawl Cymreig, 35
Cawl Llysiau Gardd, 20
Caws Pobi, 78
Cheese Cake, 66
Cig Eidion Cymreig Wedi Ei
    Frwysio, 73

Cig Moch Wedi Ei Ferwi â Saws
    Persli, 86
Cig Oen, Cig Dafad, 32
Cig Oen â Mêl, 57
Cig Oen Rhost â Saws Criafol,
    100
Clams. *See* Cregyn Gleision, 15
Cockle Cakes, 36
    Pie, 77
Cockles, 36, 77, *See also* Cregyn
    Gleision, 15
Cocos, 36
Corgimychiaid, 41
Cream Salad Dressing, 24
Cregyn Gleision, 15
Crempog, 115
    â Bwyd Môr, 115
Crempog Geirch, 53
Crempog Las, 50
Cyflaith, 118
Cyw Iâr, 113

Diod Sinsir, 54
Duck, Welsh Salt, 99. *See also*
    Pastai Ffowlyn Cymreig, 63
Dumplings, 86

Eog, 30
Eog Rhost, 97
Eve's Pudding, 63

Ffagots, 28
Fish, 104

Game Birds, Braised, 6. *See also*
    Pastai Ffowlyn Cynreig, 63
Garden Vegetable Soup, 20
Ginger Beer, 54
Gingerbread, 8
Glamorgan Sausages, 60
Golwythau Cig Dafad, 32
    Cig Oen â Phys, 32
Goose, 42
    Stuffed Roast, 42
Gower Oyster Soup, 60
Granville Sauce, 44
Griddle Cakes. *See* Welsh Cakes,
    59
Grouse. *See* Braised Game Birds
Gwin Mwyar Duon, 48
Gwlybwr Hufen, 24
Gwydd, 42

Ham, Boiled, with Parsley Sauce,
    86
    cooked with cider, 86
Harvest Cake, 107
Herrings, 1
    Potted, 53
Honey Cake, 39
Honeyed Lamb, 57
Hot-pot, 10
Hwyaden Hallt Cymreig, 99

John Dory. *See* Sgadan Aber-
    gwaun, 1

Katt Pie, 27

Lamb or Mutton, 32
    Chops, 32
    Honeyed, 57
    Saddle of, Roast, 100
    Soup. *See* Cawl Cymreig, 35
    See also Katt Pie, 27
Laver, 88
    Sauce, 88
Laverbread, 88
Lawr, 88
Leek Pasties or Turnovers, 24
Leek Tart or Flan, 82
Liver. *See* Ffagots, 28

Mackerel. *See* Sgadan Abergwaun,
    1
Mead (Metheglin), 116
Medd Hen Ffasiwn, 116
Monmouth Pudding, 111
Mother's Supper, 50
Mussel Soup, 15
    Stew, 15
Mutton. *See* Lamb or Mutton

Oatcakes: Bara Ceirch, 2
    Crempog Geirch, 53
Oatmeal Pancakes, 53
Omelette, Welsh, 50
Onion Cake, 75
Onion Sauce, 99
Oyster Soup, Gower, 60
Oysters, 60

Pancakes, 115
  Oatmeal, 53
  with Sea-food, 115
Parsley Sauce, 86
Partridge. *See* Braised Game Birds, 6
Pastai Ffowlyn Cymreig, 63
Pastai Gocos, 77
Pasteiod Cennin, 24
Pastry, 82
  short-crust, 63
  suet, 27
Pheasant. *See* Braised Game Birds, 6
Pice ar y Maen, 59
Pigeon. *See* Braised Game Birds, 6
Plate Cake, 5, 107
Potato and Apple Cake, 66
Potato Cakes, 66
Poten Bwmpen, 68
Poultry. *See* Spatchcock, 113; Welsh Chicken Pie, 63
Prawns, Prawn Paste, 41
Pumpkin, 68
  Pie, 68
Punchnep, 75
Pwdin Caws Pobi Cymreig, 94

Pwdin Efa, 65
Pwdin Eryri, 18
Pwdin Mynwy, 111
Pwdin Reis Griffiths, 12
Pwmpen, 68

Rabbit. *See* Pastai Ffowlyn Cymreig, 63
Raisin and Celery Sauce, 86
Rhubarb and Gooseberry Jam, 20
Rice Pudding, 12
Roast Fillet of Veal, 103
  Saddle of Mutton, 100
  Salmon, 97
Rowanberry Sauce (jelly), 32
Royal Icing, 80

Saddle of Mutton, Roast, 100
Salmon, 30
  Roast, 97
Saws Criafol, 32
Saws Eog Teifi, 30
Saws Nionod, 99
Saws Gwin, 18
Scallops; Scallops and Bacon, 85. *See also* Cregyn Gleision, 15
Selsig Sir Forgannwg, 60

Sgadan, 53
Sgadan Abergwaun, 1
Shrimps, Shrimp Paste, 41
Shearing Cake, 47
Snowdon Pudding, 18
Soup, Cawl, 35
  Garden Vegetable, 20
  Gower Oyster, 60
  Mussel, 15
Spatchcock, 113
Spiced Beef, 92
Spicy Apple Sauce, 42
Sponge Fingers, 71
Stewed Breast of Veal, 103
Stuffed Roast Goose, 42
Suryn Cyffaith Poeth, 103
Swper Mam, 50

Tafell O Gig Llo Rhost, 103
Tarten Gennin, 82
Tatws Rhost, 10
Teisen 'Berffro, 85
Teisen Blat, 107
Teisen Datws, 66
Teisen Fêl, 39
Teisen Galan Ystwyll, 80
Teisen Gocos, 19

Teisen Lap, 5
Teisen Nionod, 75
Torbwt Wedi Ei Fôtsio, 44
Treacle Toffee, 118
Trolennod Blawd Ceirch, 86
Trout, 104
  with Bacon, 16
Tuna. *See* Sgadan Abergwaun, 1
Turbot, Poached, 44
Twelfth Night Cake, 80

Veal, Roast Fillet of, 103
  Sauce, 103
  Stewed Breast of, 103
Vegetable Soup, Garden, 20

Welsh Braised Beef, 33
Welsh Cakes, 59
Welsh Cheese Pudding, 94
Welsh Chicken Pie, 63
Welsh Rarebit, 78
Welsh Salt Duck, 99
Welsh Veal Sauce, 103
Wholemeal Bread, 90
Wine Sauce, 18
Wyan Sir Fôn, 23
Wystrys, 60